ADORE YOUR ADOLESCENT DOG

CHANGE YOUR DOG'S FRUSTRATING BEHAVIOURS FOR LIFE

JO SELLERS

Disclaimer:

The author has provided the most accurate information possible. The techniques and training games used are science-based, and force-free based on knowledge acquired during their professional learning. The author shall not be held liable for any damages resulting from the use of this book.

Never disregard professional advice or delay in seeking it because of something you have read in this book.

Whilst every effort has been given to provide practical solutions to challenges, there is never any guarantee that these will change the behaviour. Each result is dependent on the owner doing the training and on each individual dog.

Photo credits:

Pippin Pets Dog Training

Jo Robbens Photography

Copyright © 2023 by Jo Sellers/Pippin Pets Dog Training

ISBN13 Paperback: 9798373479240

All rights reserved.

No part of this book may be reproduced in any form or by any electronic or mechanical means, including information storage and retrieval systems, without written permission from the author, except for the use of brief quotations in a book review.

CONTENTS

Introduction   9

1. WHAT IS GOING ON IN THE BRAIN   17
   What Is Adolescence?   18
   Let's Get Geeky   22
   How does all this affect our relationship with our dog?   29
   In summary   31

2. WHY I CHOOSE REWARD TRAINING AND NOT AVERSIVES   33
   Overview Of Learning Theory   34
   Effects of Aversive Methods   42
   A Note About The Old Science   45
   How To Use Reward Training In Practice   46
   Tips For Reward Training: 48

3. UNDERSTANDING YOUR DOG BY THEIR BODY LANGUAGE   53
   A Relaxed Dog   55
   What To Look Out For   57
   What to look for when dogs play together   80
   Dogs And Children   83
   Talking Dog   85

4. CREATING CALM   87
   The Stress Bucket   88
   Diet   90
   Self-Settling—Chews   90
   Rest And Sleep   92

5. BARKING 100
Why do some dogs bark more than others? 101
Coping with excessive barking 103
Excitement Barking 104
Attention Barking 104
Alert Barking 108
Doorbells and doorknocks 110
Frustration/Fear Barking 113
Distress Barking 115
Finally 116

6. JUMPING UP 118
Why Do Dogs Jump Up? 118
How to manage the jumping up 120
Teaching them to not jump up 121

7. SEXUAL MATURITY, NEUTERING AND HUMPING 127
Spaying and Neutering 128
Seasons in Females 131
False or Phantom Pregnancy 133
Chemical Castration 133
Humping 134
Just to clarify 136

8. OBJECT GUARDING 137
Management 138
Food bowls 140
Special spots on the sofa 141

9. BITING AND MOUTHING 148
Frustration 148
Overtired Or Overexcited 149
Creating Distance 149
Pain 150

Unethical Training Methods	150
What Can You Do?	150
10. INDOOR CHALLENGES	153
Counter Surfing	154
Indoor Games	156
11. COPING OUTSIDE	162
Socialisation	163
Confidence In New Environments	165
Going Past Moving Triggers	170
Meeting Other Dogs	175
Travelling In Cars	177
Walking Nicely On A Lead	179
Recalling Your Dog To Come Back To You	182
12. WHERE TO GET MORE HELP, AND USEFUL LINKS	186
How To Find A Good Trainer Or Behaviourist	187
Product Recommendations	190
About the Author	192

DEDICATION

To the most amazing dog in the world to me – Reba.

I have learnt so much from her in the years we have lived together, and it was her challenges that set me on my career path of helping other dogs.

She makes me laugh every day with her antics and her love of rolling in muck or landing in puddles. There is barely a photo of her looking clean after a walk.

To all the people who have taught me essential skills along the way, without whom I would not be able to write this book.

To my clients – past, present and future that work with me. I enjoy every single dog that I get to meet – virtual and in person.

INTRODUCTION

What Has Happened To Your Puppy?

When you chose your new puppy to come home with you, you imagined a cute bundle of fluff and lots of cuddles, who then magically became a full-size caring, quiet, loyal friend. What no one told you about is the bit in-between.

Adolescence.

The stage of your dog growing up that is painful, challenging and frustrating.

You have just managed to survive the land shark months, been to puppy classes and think you have it sussed. Oh no! It feels like it all goes wrong, your dog is 'challenging' you and you have no idea what to do about it. This period can reduce you to tears and frustration. All you want to do is smile and enjoy your dog.

There doesn't seem to be that much help out there for you. This is why I have written this book.

I will let you know what is going on in your dog's brain and explain why they are suddenly a different personality to the young pup you brought home all those months ago. Then I will take you through some of the key challenges, games and exercises you can do with your dog to regain their focus and build the relationship back up. I will enable you to manage the full-size hooligan you have into the wonderful adult dog you dreamed of.

Never forget that you are not alone, every puppy parent goes through this, and there is light at the end of the tunnel. It does get better. I've been there just like every other puppy owner.

Right now, though, you need help. It can be embarrassing taking out your dog when you are being dragged along at the other end of the lead. It can be dangerous to you and your dog. And what about those dreaded moments your oversize puppy rushes over to another group, and you cannot call them back to you? Being at home is no better as they have started barking at everything – and half of it you cannot see or hear.

Introduction

You could be feeling at the end of your tether – and even thinking of giving up your dog for rehoming. It is no surprise to hear that the most popular age of dogs being sent to rescue for rehoming is 6-24 months – the teenage period. Rescues have more 2-year-olds than any other age. More so after the recent global lockdown, and re-emergence back to work. Most arguments in households are around the dog, and how to manage them as your dog gets more out of control by the day (or hour). Adolescent dogs have caused relationship breakdowns.

I hope that this is not the case for you, but if your dog is the cause of problems at home, then all of you working together with the same games and expectations will improve home life.

Teenagers are hard work, but they do improve. The key to success? Your relationship with your dog. You may want to shout and scream, but this can only prolong the agony and ruin the precious trust you have with them.

Think about human teenagers. Do you currently have them, or have younger children that will soon be at that stage? Are you dreading this moment? How were you with your parents at that age? Relationships become precarious on both sides. The child wants more freedom and to explore new experiences, and the parent wants to keep their child safe from dangers and troubles (maybe from experience). It's a fine line to wobble on during this time. It can be a rocky path, but in (nearly) all cases, the trust returns, and everyone can breathe a sigh of relief that the teenager is now an adult.

All of the training in this book is centred around rebuilding and strengthening the trust with your dog and improving the bond you have. The games will help your dog focus on you, and both your lives will be better for this. You will coach your dog to check up on you more, and you will reward their efforts with food, praise or toys. You and your dog will be working together, not at loggerheads with each other. Harmony will be restored, and your teenager will mature into a wonderful adult that you will be proud to take out and about.

Why Should You Listen To Me?

I started Pippin Pets Dog Training in 2015 after a career in Human Resources and as a firefighter. Seeing dogs being dragged along, shouted at, or worse still hurt was painful to watch, and I knew there was a better way to teach animals. We all learn better with constructive support and being shown what to do first, and I wanted dogs to have that opportunity for success too.

I'm an Accredited Animal Training Instructor with the ABTC (Animal Behaviour and Training Council) and a

Introduction

member of the Pet Professional Guild. I studied with PACT-dogs (Professional Association of Canine Trainers) which offers high levels of reward training courses, assessing me on theory, practical skills and knowledge. Through these accreditations, I constantly keep up with the science and ethics of training to retain my accreditations and maintain the standards expected. In practical terms, I run classes for puppies, adolescent dogs, and scent training (search and sniff) and have many one-to-one clients with dogs of all ages.

I do have a special interest in Separation Anxiety (I'm a Certified Separation Anxiety Pro Trainer) as this can also affect dogs of all ages. My girl Reba suffered terribly when left home alone even for a few seconds, and this ethical method of training has transformed both our lives, and I love being able to share this with owners so that they too can have spontaneity and freedom in their lives.

So feel assured that you are in safe hands.

I will go through how you can feel better about your dog, even feeling proud - and smug – when you take them out to the local café, and they settle by your feet. What is your goal? Could it be walking past strangers in the park, and they don't have paw prints all over them from your pup? Or maybe it's just having them settle on their beds while you prepare dinner – and don't have a wet nose checking out the food on the chopping board. Imagine a calmer household...wow! Can you even dream of the time when you need to call your dog back, and they come running straight to you?

It can be achieved, and it's all about your relationship with them. How you behave around your dog influences their reactions to you, so reading this book will help you understand them better, make you less anxious and frustrated by them, and improve their responses to you.

If you follow my steps, you will have an amazing pet dog, a valued member of your family. You will love them even more as you can now live with them in harmony.

I've helped many owners get to grips with understanding why their teenage dog struggles to listen. They have implemented tips and techniques to slowly change the dog's bad habits (and their own) and have their dog want to be with them more. In my *Adore Your Adolescent* in-person classes, many times in the first week I've had dogs charging at me where the lead has been ripped out of the owner's hand, or they've been pulled off the chair when the dog has suddenly needed to run and explore the field. But by the sixth week, all the dogs are walking around calmly in close proximity, less interested in the others and only have eyes on their humans. No more falling off chairs. Success! Owners have learnt many new skills to keep their dogs

Introduction

interested so the lead walking and recall improve. It is after this class that I tend to be given most chocolate as a thank you! But my greatest prize is seeing the smiles on all the human faces – and the dogs too.

In this book, I will start with what is going on in the brain of your teenage dog – it's quite fascinating but key also to understand why they do what they do at this life stage. They go through a huge developmental phase, with twists and turns, and knowing what is going on helps you forgive their cheekiness (I don't like to use the term naughty as they are only being dogs). I explain why I use reward training and not aversive methods that promise quick fixes but ruin your dog, and the importance of learning their body language.

The next section then covers all those pesky challenging behaviours from barking to countertop surfing, lead walking to recall games, and more. Each part will describe the struggle, and provide you with games, management tips and exercises to help teach your dog to change what they do to something a bit more agreeable for us humans to tolerate.

The final section is about recognising the struggles, when you feel overwhelmed, and where to go for more help. It can be very daunting to feel you have to work on everything, so pick the most important couple of topics, practice these first and come back to the less important deal breakers later. Sometimes your dog just has more going on in their head than we can manage, so knowing when to refer and whom to go to is explained, especially if there is more severe aggression or guarding behaviours being displayed.

Safety has to come first in all of these exercises so do a check on where you are training especially outdoors, and consult professionals if you are in any way concerned.

Want to learn how to *Adore Your Adolescent*? Turn the page now and dive right in.

1
WHAT IS GOING ON IN THE BRAIN

Wondering why your puppy's behaviour has suddenly become erratic?

First things first, your puppy is not broken. Not even close. This is normal development for them. I repeat, normal. So don't despair. Adolescence happens to every dog, with no exceptions. But if this is normal, why are they suddenly so different to the bundle of puppies you had yesterday? You know, the puppy you were just starting to understand and in return was beginning to listen to you. Now you may as well be on another planet.

Before you can even start to help your dog to navigate the adolescent months, it helps to understand what is going on inside their head. Without getting into why they are behaving the way they are, you really will struggle to be successful in fine-tuning those pesky annoying new habits and will end up damaging your hard-earned relationship with them.

In this chapter, I will go through some of the findings of the teenage brain, and summarise what is going on. This will help you to appreciate the inner turmoil, which in turn will even help your dog mature quicker. I have read, listened and absorbed many research studies, but have not quoted or cited individual articles or research projects here. Instead, I will give you the key points and how it applies to your dog. So let's dive into it.

What Is Adolescence?

Simply put, this is the term applied to mammals when they change from babies to adults. In humans, it's the teenage years, but you will be pleased to know that in dogs, the changes happen quicker, and therefore they mature much quicker than your children. Generally, it starts to take effect from around 5 months and can be until over two years, depending on many factors including the size or breed of your dog (or mix). Smaller dogs tend to develop quicker than larger breeds, but that does not mean you are off the hook, they will still be a teenager.

As with humans, dogs need to go through this phase of adjustment to become an adult, and it is the time of most upheaval in a dog's brain. Many biological processes are happening, and these can result in some very frustrating behaviours. Being able to understand these processes will help you not only cope, but deal with these extra challenges.

Your dog will still be physically growing, getting taller, forming complex bone joints, building more muscle to become stronger, and these changes can be a bit more obvious and forgiving. However, the brain also is still under construction.

It can be very easy to assume that the brain is static – it is a formed structure that just grows bigger to fit the increasing skull size, and what you teach them in their early months is carefully stored and easily accessed at all times – you assume that what they learnt first surely must stay there. If you spent time teaching a puppy a cue, then how can they forget to apply the learning when you ask them again?

In reality, the brain that the puppy was born with was just temporary, and more building is needed to help your dog live in your world. Adolescence allows this redesign of their most important organ, but it cannot cope with changing all at once, so different parts of the brain mature at different times and speeds. This is why teenage dogs struggle to make good decisions, show self-control or remember any previous training they did. Their emotions can run high as the control centre for these takes a while longer to develop.

Your dog will reach sexual maturity long before they are socially mature, which is very common in mammals. They may be able to have puppies themselves, but they are still very bad at assessing risks, decision-making, problem-solving and focus are nearly non-existent. Like humans, teenagers can become pregnant (or get someone else pregnant), but do not have the maturity to be in charge of a weapon like a car on our roads. Even when older teenagers can legally drive, they are far from mentally fully formed for risk/responsibility which is why their insurance is so high and they are more likely to have accidents.

The last part of the brain to develop is the emotional centre, where reward/punishment cognition is formed. This can explain those random tantrums at the smallest frustration. Has your dog ever squeaked or squealed at you if you are not fast enough to attend to their immediate needs? You are not alone!

A word of caution...

We have to be careful not to anthropomorphise (confession time – I cannot say, let alone spell, this word! To dog geeks I say 'that anthro-thingy' but normally avoid this word altogether!). It means we put all our human characteristics such as thoughts, feelings, behaviours, emotions and values onto another species, which just is not the case and can cause a lot of problems for our dogs – our understandings and expectations are off kilter by miles. Other species are not human, they are different and we should respect this. It's like saying chimps are the same as humans – we share the majority of our DNA from common ancestors, but we are still very different. We have different skills, thinking, values and language.

Same for domesticated dogs. They may have shared a common ancestor with ancient wolves, but they are no more the same as modern wolves as we are to apes. So assuming dogs are the same as us is even more off the mark.

When it comes to studying adolescence in domesticated dogs, research is limited but it is a growing area of interest. The challenge is to be able to interpret the results by deducing the dog's body language. Many studies do not have a large enough group of participants, and many rely on the owner's assumptions instead of independent observers. Others have no control group, or the methodology applied is not rigorous enough. All is not quite lost.

There has been much more research on human adolescents and the advantage is the comprehension and language which is easier for scientists to interpret, as well as the ability to scan the brain. Other species have been studied, and there are quite a lot of similarities to the developing brain of mammals, but it is predominantly human brains that our research information comes from. We need to take the common themes and apply this carefully to dogs. But dogs are not humans. However, we can take the similarities to understand the growth and development of the brain, how it sheds some bits, grows other bits, and become the final adult control centre.

Let's Get Geeky

The neurobiology of the adolescent brain is fascinating, and several developmental stages happen that alter the structure and the functions of the brain.

With your young puppy, not all of the brain is working. Some sections are on pause, waiting for the rise of the hormones to trigger them into action. This enables just the key areas to develop and grow, enough to enable them to make sense of their world. Areas to develop first are the olfactory area (the sniffing and smelling spots), heat detection (so that they can find their mum aka food source), and then the other senses. While their senses are improving, they are concentrating on working out what is safe, whom to hang out with, and understanding all these things (living beings and objects) that are around them. It's quite a lot for them, so to make sure the most important parts of the brain are focused, other areas are on hold until the puppy is older.

As your pup approaches the 6-month age, key changes happen. With the onset of adolescence, hormones are released into the body to kick start further development beginning with the pause button being released.

When the dog's brain has been scanned, it does look different to ours. The main front part, the frontal cortex, is smaller in proportion to the rest of the brain and has fewer ridges and smaller folds, so the frontal lobes have less surface area, and the cerebral cortex is thinner too. The frontal lobes play an important role in planning and decision-making, hence why dogs have limited ability in these areas compared to humans.

Based on human research, the teenage phase is where the most dramatic growth spurts happen in the brain. New thinking skills are developed which ultimately become the decision-making maturity of adults. Right now, as with your dog, the thinking is still strongly influenced by emotions, overriding the ability to be rational.

The basal functions which sit near the back of the brain get to be upgraded first, and emotional control is among this cluster. A basal area is a group of structures that allow connections to be made so that parts of the brain can work together. It manages the signals for movement from the brain to muscles, so very important for a vulnerable young puppy.

Within the basal area is the limbic system, an area that is involved with the emotional and behavioural responses, including key survival instincts such as feeding, reproduction and fight/flight responses. This also explains why dogs become sexually mature long before they are socially or mentally mature. Teenagers both of the human and dog variety experience intense emotions as this part of the brain develops. But the section of the brain that should be controlling emotions is further down the list to be upgraded, hence why 'teenage outbursts' are common. Feelings are more urgent and more intense, and impulsive decisions are often made without any logical thinking applied. Relying on the limbic system for reactions does not result in calm decisions being made.

The frontal part of the brain which is responsible for controlling impulsive reactions develops later, and the prefrontal cortex is last in line. This section impacts the moderation of behaviour in social situations, personality traits and decision-making. Think of it in car terms: the teenager can put their foot on the accelerator, but there is no brake pedal, yet...

If that isn't enough, there is also another process happening – the use it or lose it principle, or in technical terms, plasticity. Not everything the puppy started with will stay into adulthood – in brain terms. Some neural connections are weakened as they are not needed as much, and others are strengthened as the brain becomes more efficient. Some brain cells are lost forever, but others grow in new areas as needed. As vital body function controls are at the back of the brain, again, the changes start here first, and the pre-frontal cortex is last, again. For this reason, adults have the necessary wiring to spot mistakes in decisions made, teenagers literally can't notice these things.

Starting to get a better understanding of what your dog is going through? It's not finished yet.

Another key change happening at this time is the development of receptors for the hormone oxytocin, often called the bonding hormone. This can explain the neediness in teenage dogs, and the regular reassurance and connection to their caregiver, despite the desire for independence.

As you can see, the teenage brain goes through a massive reorganisation, and parts of the brain are not properly connecting or communicating with each other resulting in more impulsive actions, emotional reactions and being prone to take risks as consequences of actions are not in the thought process yet.

A common misconception is that your dog has become stubborn, and maybe you feel you need to 'tell it off' or punish the action. In reality, your dog is not stubborn but just confused, and unable to control itself. They cannot help it. The effect of this is one day not responding to recall, suddenly unable to walk slowly on the lead, or starting to jump on guests again. Their brain is not processing the original training cue as before, as the connections are all reorganising themselves. Everything is one jumbled mess. Knowing now what is going on in their heads, no wonder. Imagine trying to study a technical piece of text for work while on a building site – you just cannot concentrate or take in the right bits of information.

You may also think that your dog is now choosing to ignore you, and won't listen anymore. As puppies, you are their world as they are guided through the sights and noises of our living. However, teenage dogs start to realise that there is a bigger world out there which is enticing. One key hormone is testosterone, and this gives them more confidence to explore and become bolder.

Dogs smell the world first; they have an amazing capacity to detect molecules and get lots of information at a microscopic level. A third of their brain is just for scent detection, and so their brain is incredibly busy processing all this information around them. Hearing is much lower down in the sensory pecking order, so often their sense of smell overrides everything else. They are not deliberately ignoring you; they are not hearing you. If they are concentrating on figuring out their surroundings, you bellowing their name is just a distraction from their main job of sniffing. Multi-tasking is not high on the sensory agenda, and they find it hard to concentrate on too many things at once. Waiting for them to finish sniffing that spot before you try and distract them is going to give you more success in getting them to listen to you.

As mentioned before, there is limited research on the brain development of young dogs compared to human teenagers, but behaviours are quite similar. Teenage dogs are unable to process information like mature dogs and often engage in risky behaviours. The frontal cortex is not yet registering risk, or able to limit impulsive reactions, so the brain can only go with the stronger urge of immediate reward. And then we throw in breed-specific traits such as the need to chase rabbits!

Some studies have even shown that males take more risks than females in social settings. Both become pickier about whom they want to hang out with, which can lead to more dog/dog aggression. In humans, young children will be best friends with everyone in their class, making for some huge birthday parties. As they go through the teens, they make new friends but it's a smaller gang of trusted individuals. Finally, as adults, we find it much harder to make new friends and keep to just a handful of special people that we can confide in and have fun with. The same applies to dogs too – confident puppies play with most other puppies they meet, adolescents will still play, but start to be selective, and by the time they are adults, they may avoid most strange dogs but only play with their small network of best friends. There are always exceptions, but most follow this same pattern.

With self-control low down on the agenda, and more emotional urges, adolescent dogs show much more hormonal reactive behaviours than adult dogs. The need for instant reward and gratification is pronounced compared to puppies, and more risks are taken.

Phew, this is exhausting but it hasn't stopped for our gorgeous adolescent dogs.

From about 6 months to approximately 14 months (or so), your dog has a sensitive period. Similar to their puppy fear period at 8-12 weeks, this essential growing phase develops as your dog explores more. It's a safety/survival thing to keep them safe while they venture further from their home, or you. In teenage dogs, rather than one solid state it comes and goes like waves and you may notice one week your dog is fine, and the next being spooked by the same thing they encounter.

How does all this affect our relationship with our dog?

Adolescence is a normal stage of development that can leave you feeling like you have lost your dog, or want to pull your hair out. You have not failed as a dog guardian or failed at their training. Younger puppies seem so simple when faced with challenges, but now the problems seem so much more complex as your dog matures. Your wonderful dog is turning into a hooligan, and you may not love them as much – or feel like you can live with them. Your relationship is at stake, and you could be feeling embarrassed taking them out in public. Every puppy owner goes through this however it is not often talked about in detail, almost like a taboo secret. No one is keen to admit just how tough this life stage is. But it is temporary.

As long as you remember that your dog's brain is under construction, and appreciate all the physiological, emotional, physical and hormonal changes they are going through. It's not stubbornness, and you just need to be super patient and keep training simple. Help build new connections by remaining calm, and not getting frustrated with them.

Your relationship with your teenage dog is critical for helping them out of adolescence. Studies have shown that the stronger the relationship, the quicker they mature. If your bond is strong, it will be easier to see the light at the end of the teenage tunnel.

It can be tempting to fall into despair and frustration, and even want to give up on your dog. It's at this age that many dogs get rehomed. Moving to a rescue centre at this critical development stage can have profound long-term effects on their adult behaviour. Equally, using punishment-based training methods or aversive equipment can be damaging too, as their tolerance to stress is reduced while the brain reforms.

You can feel like all your efforts are not working, and you can become more disengaged from your dog. Why train them if they are not listening? Without your help, they really cannot learn the adult habits we want them to have.

They are not being disobedient, so do not give up on them now. Count to 10 (several times if needed), take a deep breath, and instead of getting annoyed, ask yourself what you can teach your dog to do instead that will help them learn and remember...and what will help your sanity. This phase will pass. I promise.

Having a strong bond throughout the adolescent phase is essential for their growth. The weaker your relationship with them, the more the conflict with them cannot be resolved and the shouting or any aversives used can be damaging long term. Focus on how you interact with your dog and maintain the quality of the relationship for the first few years of your time with them. Build the trust first, then worry about obedience – recall is essential, but the rest can come later.

Struggles with the relationship can be a two-way thing. Adolescent mammals are pre-programmed to seek out conflict with their caregiver. They test the boundaries and then re-engage. This means that your dog may not listen to you but will hang on to every word of a stranger. This can be annoying, but it will pass and as long as you keep calm, your bond will be back stronger than ever. Is there a change in your routine that may help your dog cope better?

In summary

As your puppy transitions from youngster to adult during adolescence, its world is chaotic. You have read just how much their brain is changing. It's phenomenal and no wonder they can become a problematic pet. Undesirable behaviours intensify and your dog is more unpredictable and frustrated, leading you to become more unpredictable to them, and frustrated. Not a great combination. This makes it hard for your puppy to adjust.

There are so many hormonal changes going on, that it is a tough time for both of you. It is only a phase, albeit a challenging one, but it will get better.

By just understanding what it is they are going through and using compassion, patience and calmness, you are helping them become tolerant and resilient adult dogs and become the best versions of themselves. And a happy home for you. You will have a dog to be insanely proud of.

2

WHY I CHOOSE REWARD TRAINING AND NOT AVERSIVES

There are so many methods to use to train a dog, but not all are kind, ethical, or appropriate. But that doesn't stop some owners and trainers from using them. How do you know what to do, or what works?

You don't need to surf YouTube far to find so many different trainers, using various techniques, to perform that magic fix on your dog. But is it all as it seems?

In this chapter, I am going to outline the style of training I use, why I don't use others, and why there is often confusion around the learning theory for training mammals.

You have read in the last chapter just how sensitive your dog is at this crucial stage of its development. And the key to maintaining any type of sanity is your relationship with your dog. Training them should be a joy, as well as a necessity, and not be damaging to their mental well-being. Constant, unpredictable stress on your dog is not helping their brain development in the best way and has long-term effects on them as an adult dog. What they are learning now will stick with them for a very long time indeed.

The dog training industry is as yet unregulated, so no one is breaking the law by any methods they use, but there are big differences in standards and approaches to welfare. Some accredited bodies are driving high standards in terms of up-to-date scientific knowledge and application, and ensuring animal welfare and understanding is at the core of any method used (ABTC is one of the best for this, and I am proud to be accredited by them—they also make their members accountable). But anyone can operate as a trainer without even learning the basics of how to train an animal.

Overview Of Learning Theory

Do read this section, as it can help you understand some of the methods you see, and some of the terminology that can be used. And it's the misconceptions and misinterpretations of the terminology that leads to lots of confusion. This is a huge topic, but I will attempt to give you enough of a summary that does not make your brain hurt, but can make you a bit more mindful of what you are doing and the impact on your dog. The theory is not just for dogs, but all mammals, including humans.

Theory One

Dogs sometimes have a natural response to things – such as drooling when they smell food. We also have these and you may wonder why you automatically jump when you get tapped on the shoulder. These responses are built in, and we can make these responses happen to new events/noises etc. if they are paired together. This is classical conditioning (learning by natural reflexes).

An example could be that your dog loves cheese, and drools at the smell of cheese. The cheese is kept in the fridge. The noise of the fridge door means nothing to your dog until you go there to get out some cheese to give your dog. Your dog is drooling at the cheese. Soon, if you repeat this often enough, your dog has paired the sound of the fridge door with the thought of cheese, even if you have run out of the stuff, and will drool at just the sound of the fridge door opening.

Using this theory in the context of dog training, a dog learns a response to what was meaningless beforehand. The lead to a puppy is nothing until it learns that if you pick it up, they get to go out and play. Your dog continues to get excited at the sight of the lead – they have learnt that association. Not all items mean nice things happen. Maybe they had a scary encounter at the vets, with the specific smell of the reception area. Now each time they smell that special cleaning solution used at vets, they start to panic even though nothing has happened to them.

Dogs are learning associations all the time, and your adolescent dog is relearning new responses to their environment and humans around them. Things they learnt before can be changed, as the brain connections morph and grow during the teenage months.

Theory Two

There are other ways to train your dog, and this is to teach a response to a specific cue, also known as Operant Learning (learning by thinking). The diagram below shows the main terminology used, but to be honest, there are many more factors in play than just these four.

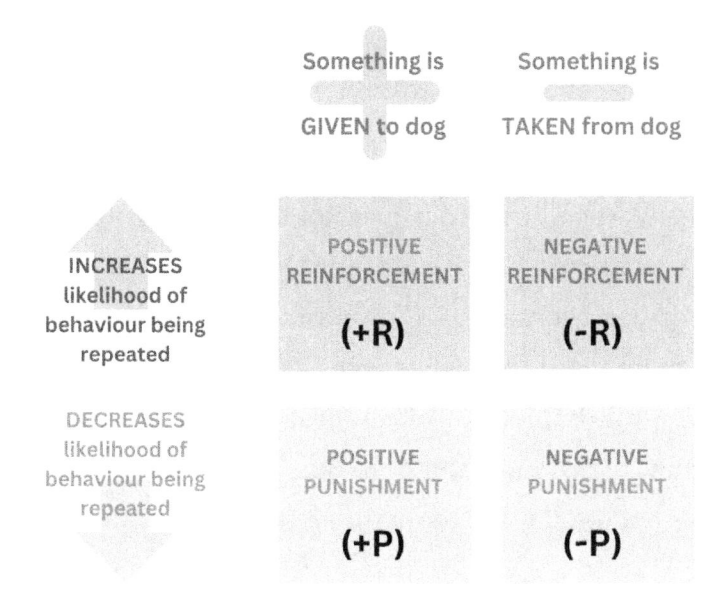

	Something is GIVEN to dog	Something is TAKEN from dog
INCREASES likelihood of behaviour being repeated	POSITIVE REINFORCEMENT (+R)	NEGATIVE REINFORCEMENT (-R)
DECREASES likelihood of behaviour being repeated	POSITIVE PUNISHMENT (+P)	NEGATIVE PUNISHMENT (-P)

Contingency Table of Operant Learning

In psychological terms, positive, negative, reinforcement and punishment have different meanings to the way we use them in general conversations.

To start with, positive and negative do not mean good or bad. Your idea of good may be another person's perception of bad anyway. And for dog training, we need to remember that it is not your views, but the dog's view that matters.

When it comes to learning, positive means to add something, and negative is to remove something. And reinforcement is not based on value, but on increasing the frequency of a behaviour or action. Punishment then is not as we know it such as a physical application of pain or mental restrictions that the receiver finds aversive, but the decreasing of frequency of a behaviour.

It is good to note that a trainer will not just operate in one of the boxes only. Life is just not as simple as that, and as owners, you too have a choice as to which boxes you will be more biased towards. Using all of the methods will eventually teach your dog what you want them to do but some have undesirable side effects from certain methods used. Nothing is in total isolation, but I will explain the differences and help you choose for yourself.

I am very biased towards the Positive Reinforcement box – i.e. I give a reward to the dog for doing as I asked, but I will also set boundaries, and even yank my dog's lead if she suddenly turns towards the road while walking with me – you have to react to a life/death emergency, safety is paramount. However, with reward training, the chance of her bouncing into oncoming traffic is minimised by encouraging and rewarding her to stay closer to me, which she chooses to do.

In reward training, we are adding something really good like some tasty chicken, or a game of tug, as a reward for doing what we are asking them. We hope that there is enough of a 'pay' for your dog to keep doing the action. This is positive reinforcement and is scientifically proven to be a very effective, kind, more humane and easy-to-use way to train your dog. The dog is guided and encouraged to do an action and rewarded to motivate them to increase the chance to do it again.

However, this is not a quick fix but a way to create a new habit; nothing is quick, and expectations should be set for the owner to appreciate this. Consistency and repetition will lead to stronger behaviour, and as there is no fear or intimidation, your bond with your dog will be strong. As we saw in Chapter 1, the relationship with your dog is the most precious thing to hold onto during adolescence.

It is important to find out your dog's motivations, and they may be different depending on what you are asking your dog to do, and the environment they are in at that time. Each toy or type of food has a preference. What do you go for first in a buffet? It may not be the same as the person with you. Just giving a tiny dry treat may not motivate your dog to repeat that behaviour, especially a recall past many distractions!

Once you have built up a strong habit of responding to the cue, and your dog has learnt it well, then you can drop down to occasionally rewarding with food/games for the best efforts, but for easy things such as a sit, smiling and praise may well be enough. I save the food for recall – that is a lifesaving skill that I want my dog to be super motivated to do regardless of where she is.

The flip side is Negative Punishment, but that does not mean I apply any force or pain onto the dog. The way I encourage my clients to do this is to ignore when the dog is doing something I don't like – but there are caveats. If the dog is jumping up at me for attention, then I remove my focus away from them. So I am taking away my attention (negative) in the likelihood that the dog will stop jumping on me (punishment to decrease the jumping).

I strongly feel that just ignoring your dog will lead to carnage and chaos – you wouldn't leave them to climb on the kitchen counter to eat food scraps. It is important to consider what you want your dog to do instead, use a lot of positive reinforcement to teach them what you want them to do, and reward heavily. In the jumping example just given, I would not leave a dog to just jump constantly on visitors. I would set them up in advance to have treats on the floor – if their nose is down, they can't jump up – and manage the environment using staYgates or have them on a lead and only let them approach the visitor when they were calmer. Using management techniques is key to restricting their ability to keep repeating an unwanted habit.

Remember, sometimes we are actively rewarding your dog, but they can also self-reward – it's their view of what is good that counts. Jumping up at the kitchen counter gives them food prizes, even if you are not in the room at the time. Again, management of shutting doors, using stairgates, or supervising them is better than repeatedly going through the cycle of your dog being cheeky, and you then shouting at them. Break that pattern.

The last two boxes are ones that I will rarely visit – unless it is a life/death scenario and I have had to grab my dog in an emergency. But I try and be mindful to not use them. Balanced trainers are those that reward the dog with one hand, but then use aversive methods and gadgets at the same time. They often offer a quick fix – but when you are changing habits and behaviours, there is no such thing.

In brief, Positive Punishment is to add something in the hope of decreasing the behaviour and often shock collars (electric collars), sprays, prong (spikes on the inside) collars that tighten around the dog or even ranting and shouting at your dog all fall into this category. Pain is put on the dog to 'stop' them from doing something such as pulling on the lead.

Negative Reinforcement is the moment that the shock or prong pressure is released. The thinking is for the dog to find relief so they won't do the thing that started the pain.

Effects of Aversive Methods

Science has shown that there are a lot of flaws and problems that can occur using these methods. Excessive stress has been shown to inhibit learning and this can have a significant impact on what and how our dogs learn.

Firstly, we covered how dogs learn by association. If you are applying a shock, because the dog pulled on the lead, in your mind you are linking the pull of the lead to the shock. But what if your dog was looking at a pushchair at the time? Your dog is most likely to associate the pushchair with the pain. So next time they see a pushchair, they are more likely to freak out as they have connected the pain to it and the shock/spikes/scary noise will follow. And then they will probably pull on the lead to get more distance from the pushchair, so you apply the shock. It can be a downward spiral.

Next, if these gadgets were the magic solution that worked, then they should only be needed once or twice. However, users have to keep upping the pain or pressure, as the dog can get used to the 'entry' level of discomfort. Also, trying things such as spraying water in the dog's face can be horrible for some, but hugely fun for others.

Finally, and most seriously, if you use force or pain to suppress behaviour, you have not taught your dog what they are allowed to do instead. So like a ticking bomb, it is bubbling up in them as you have not worked to create new habits. And it will explode – and worse than before. It may not be the same behaviour as the one you were trying to stop, but it is likely to be an equally damaging alternative.

An important consideration is also the effect of the constant 'no, no, no', with the dog getting rather despondent as they do not understand what they can do. They can't read our minds, and if there is no coaching then they will give up. They become shut down, a condition called 'learned helplessness'. They don't try anything, as nothing rewards them.

When using reward training, the mindset is different for the dog. With traditional training (more punishment in the literal sense), the dog learns that unless the handler specifically says so, the dog is wrong at all other times, and it freezes. The advantage of reward training is that we encourage the dog to be creative and to try new moves in the hope that will make the reward happen.

By becoming a dog that is keen to try, more complex tricks and behaviours can be taught much more easily. So instead of freezing, the dog can enjoy learning.

Another serious consideration that affects me and how I train dogs is the fact that we have domesticated dogs who become very reliant on us and vulnerable. In human society, access to vulnerable humans is regulated and monitored. How you interact with them is carefully controlled. Yet our dogs are even more vulnerable as they are not humans but dependent on us. Using aversive methods on them in my opinion feels like an abuse of the vulnerable and should not be tolerated in a dog-loving society.

To me, using leads that tighten around their necks, jerking the lead to lift them off their paws, shocking them or using painful gadgets are aligned with being abusive and can only terrify and intimidate the receiver of these methods.

In my heart, I feel much better if I can teach my dog what to do, not need to shout (unless in an extreme emergency) and allow her to feel safe and relaxed around me. Our relationship is the core of living happily with each other, and I want this for you and your dog too.

So, when you are choosing the method to train your dog, have a serious think about the impact it will have on them.

If you have been shown or watched a video of a way to get your dog to do something, does it feel right in your gut? Are you comfortable repeating that action towards your dog? Dogs have feelings and fears, so if you have any doubts, then be prepared to walk away and do more research on alternatives.

A Note About The Old Science

Back in 1947, Schenkel wrote a study paper about captive wolves, and this was put into the more public domain in 1970 when the thought was that an Alpha was in charge and had priority over every other wolf. The study was about a group of unrelated individuals caged in a small captive area, and this was then deemed to show 'normal wolf behaviour'. Fights, who ate first, who slept where were assumed to be then normal for all wolves—wild or captive.

But we learnt before that domestic dogs are not wolves. It's the same as assuming a chimp 'Big Brother' dictates how we humans lead our lives. This science was redacted, withdrawn, and disbanded but sadly still is the basis for many ill-informed dog trainers today.

There is no place for dominance, alphas, shoving a dog on its back, thinking dogs will take over if they eat before us and so on. If you find a trainer or a video that goes on about these terms, then walk away – no, run! They are about fifty years behind in science.

There is no excuse to intimidate or dominate our beloved pet dogs.

Much more validated science is out there to promote a partnership, a strong bond and trust with our four-legged friends. I much prefer to set the dog up for success by teaching them the boundaries and what we would like from them, rather than setting them up for failure so I can shout at them and they are confused about what it is they should be doing.

How To Use Reward Training In Practice

Reward training is about asking your dog to do something, them doing the thing and being praised or rewarded for doing it. They learn that actions = consequences, and we can use pleasant consequences such as yummy food to encourage that particular action.

The sequence is ……. Ask – Do – Mark – Reward

<u>Ask</u>

This is called the cue – it is a word, noise, whistle pips, or hand gesture that is unique to a specific behaviour or action, that you have taught your dog to associate together. Command to me sounds rather bullish, but it is the same thing.

<u>Do</u>

This is your dog responding to the cue, and if you have practised enough, should be happening quickly and most times. They are a dog with their own brain, so 100%

response all the time is a dream, rather than reality. But up nearer 90% is good enough for most dogs most of the time.

Mark

To teach your dog that the move they have done is the right one, marking the split second of the right position with a unique special one-syllable word or click of the clicker tells your dog they have done well. The clicker is great as it is the same sound regardless of who in the family is holding it, and it is quick and precise. If I don't have a clicker on me, I use the word 'Yip', but I've heard clients say 'Boom', 'Wow', or other variations. Be mindful of not only the volume of voice you use but your body position – leaning over your dog can be seen as intimidating, so stand up straight.

Reward

To encourage them to do the action or behaviour again, and increase the frequency of them repeating it, then a great reward boosts the chances. One measly dry biscuit won't be enough for most dogs, so you need to first think generous, and more importantly, what does _your_ dog perceive to be the best reward?

When learning something new or difficult, you bring out the big guns – chicken, frankfurters, the best tug toy or whatever your dog loves most. My girl loves cooked broccoli and blueberries. But these can squish in your pocket.

All dogs need to eat, but dogs may not want to have a food reward in all situations. If they are slightly stressed, or racing about, then they will not want food in their stomachs. My girl is a foodie, so my life is quite easy. But dogs can be motivated more by games or connections to you. Is there a special squeaky tug toy that you can use for a recall reward? Most dogs do not value your touch as much as you think, and not when outside.

You can even use the environment as your reward. After some excellent walking, maybe let them sniff the fences on your route or let them go and run around chasing birds after a speedy recall back to you in the park. It doesn't always have to be food given to the dog that is a reward.

Try different things, and see in which situation your dog responds to different rewards.

Tips For Reward Training:

Tip One

If your dog is learning something new, then I would only start with a hand gesture as this is easiest for dogs to follow – they find language the hardest so I only introduce this once they have learnt what it is you want them to do.

To do this, I use food in my hand by the dog's nose and can move my hand around to get the dog to follow and reposition its body. A sit can be taught by holding a treat by their nose, lifting your hand a few centimetres so their head tilts up, and this makes their bottom flop down. You then mark the second their bottom hits the floor. And give the food.

After a couple of turns with food in your hand, then you pretend to hold the food. Have your hand in the same position, do the same action, and you will get the same response. Mark and then reach for the food and give it to your dog.

If they are responding the first time to 80% of asking once, then add in your verbal/noise cue – say the word 'sit' just before you then do the hand gesture, and don't forget to mark and treat after. That way, they will learn to associate the word with the action and you will get the response you want.

Tip Two

Are you too keen and saying the cue word while your dog has no idea what you want them to do? Then they will associate your cue with whatever they are doing at the time you say it. They are responding to the word, but not in the way you anticipated. If you are just repeatedly saying 'sit', while they are sniffing the ground, then they will just sniff whenever you say 'sit'. If this happens, don't just keep doing/saying the same thing; their response won't change. Go back to find out why it isn't working for you both anymore. Maybe you jumped into a difficult environment too quickly, or maybe you have not practised enough. With an adolescent dog, maybe the hormones have fogged up the brain. Go back to basics, and teach the action again, possibly even using a new cue word.

Tip Three

Take care to use a separate cue for each action, so that nothing has a double meaning. Using their name can often make us lazy and we say their name to mean look at me, come to me, leave that, get off the sofa etc. So their name becomes white noise as your dog has no clue what you are asking of them. And this is why your teenage dog can be seen to be ignoring you. Rather than getting frustrated, stop, and think carefully about if you are being clear with your instructions and cues.

Once they have learnt the action and respond well to the cue, you can change your reward to one that is fairly rewarding but not the top thing. An example is that now, my dog responds reliably to sitting. I don't give a food reward now, but maybe a smile or verbal praise. But, for recall and one where she has gone past some distractions, I will still give her several pieces of tasty food for the huge effort she made. If she is learning a new skill, top rewards are there for her. Don't be stingy or too quick to give up the top-value rewards, or your dog will lose motivation to listen and respond to you.

Tip Four

Dogs learn best when they are in a safe environment, so when you do any of the exercises, start by teaching them indoors at home. Get the responses good before you then practice it in your garden, where you have all the wind and wildlife smells around them. Slowly get other family members to move around at a distance while you practice.

Eventually, you will then be able to start training outside in the more distracting environments. Start with familiar places and build up to new parks or beaches, and more distractions. Set realistic expectations too – if your dog is great in the kitchen at running to you on a recall cue, it is unlikely for them to next week run past lots of dogs and picnics and go straight to you. All learning takes time so build up steadily.

If you are unsure, or if there are any big distractions, then put them on a harness and attach a long line holding the other end, so that they cannot run off and repeat bad habits.

When going out with my dog and we visit somewhere new, she is on a 3-metre lead which allows her a bit of freedom to sniff but is easy for me to hold without getting tangled. Once the beaches start to fill up with picnics and children's toys, or we are walking in new areas and I'm unsure of hazards, I will use this longer lead.

And of course, all dogs should be on a lead near livestock fields. Do not think your dog will be okay – temptation and instinct are huge, so management is the only way to go. Your dog is an opportunistic hunter, and even the most laid-back cuddly fluffball will revert to hunting if the temptation is enough – those sheep are irresistible to them. Farmers will and do shoot dogs as they need to protect their animals. Don't let your dog be one of them. Be sensible, and realistic and you will be fine.

3

UNDERSTANDING YOUR DOG BY THEIR BODY LANGUAGE

Half the battle to get your dog through its adolescence is the ability to understand them. You expect them to interpret and respond to your language, but how much effort are you making to truly understand their communication back to us? In this chapter, I will go through some of the key body language to look out for and why this could be important for you both.

Through their domestication, dogs have become masters of understanding humans. They have learned to interpret our tone of voice to expect nice or scary, and the tiny twitches in our facial features also help them decipher what will happen – are you asking them to move, or are they worried about what will happen next? Humans have bred dogs to enhance or change their physical features, but did you know that they have also evolved to help you understand them by mobilising their eyebrows so they can make that 'baby eyes' face? Incredible. They have even changed how they look to make things easier and yet most owners are not very good at spotting, and interpreting, all their language.

A lot of research has gone into what the range of feelings are for dogs, how they express them through their bodies (and barks), and how you can interpret them to the situation. Dogs are highly unlikely to have all the same complex feelings that you have – the guilt look is one. Dogs don't have the same plans/intentions and therefore to them, right and wrong are very different. They do what works for them and avoid what doesn't work for them. If they have done something, they don't then sit there and think about any remorse for damage – life is not like that for them. It's owners that come into the home, horror on our faces and raised voices that sets them to look appeasing – trying to calm the situation and hopefully have not had to learn to run and hide from you. They are not planning or plotting to overthrow the human race, they may be sneaky for grabbing treats, but not malicious.

With all body language, you can only best guess the meaning of each look but you need to consider the context at that moment – where are they, what has just been seen or happened, what is around them at the time, and what danger do they perceive to be imminent?

Looking at the context and lead-up to the event is key to working out most adolescent behaviours. Think of an action having a body language consequence. You cannot just look at the body language without considering the background and environment too.

I will go through some of the most common signs, and give a small explanation about them, but this list is not exhaustive, nor will all dogs show all of these in the same situations. Each dog needs to be looked at as an individual, and some 'whispering' behaviours may no longer be expressed as the dog has learnt that if these have been ignored, they move straight on to the 'screaming' end of the scale.

In this chapter, I will go through the various parts of a dog's body and how they use these in communication to show if they are happy or worried.

A Relaxed Dog

To start with, you need to know what your relaxed dog looks like, so you understand changes more easily.

Starting with the body and face, it should look relaxed. There is no tension and their hair is looking normal – no standing on end on the top of their bodies.

Learn what your dog's natural tail carriage is. It is good to learn about other breeds too so that you are not misinterpreting a different tail position in another dog. Pugs and Shiba Inu's (just to name a tiny few) have very curly tails. They sit high on the back and curl around. Some dogs such as Poodles have straighter tails, but the normal carriage is up in the air pointing to the sky. Whippets and Greyhounds carry their tails very low and often tucked up under between the back legs. And then you have the Labradors and Spaniels whose tails just droop and flick up at the end, like a smile.

Relaxed tail positions

Once you know your dog, then anything different will alert you to their mood. But knowing what is normal for other dog breeds will help you when you encounter other dogs out and about.

What To Look Out For

Remember, to be able to interpret your dog's communications, look at the environment, what is happening, and even what has been happening leading up to that moment. It's all about the context. The 'ladder of aggression' overleaf gives an idea of some of the things to look out for, and I will go into more detail as well. Dogs start at the bottom of the ladder with the green and build up with their communication signals. But, be warned, if the whispers don't get listened to, then your dog may move straight to the yellow or red zones at the top. It's not like feelings get automatically reset to neutral after each event, especially if no one is listening to you.

The Canine 'Ladder of Aggression'

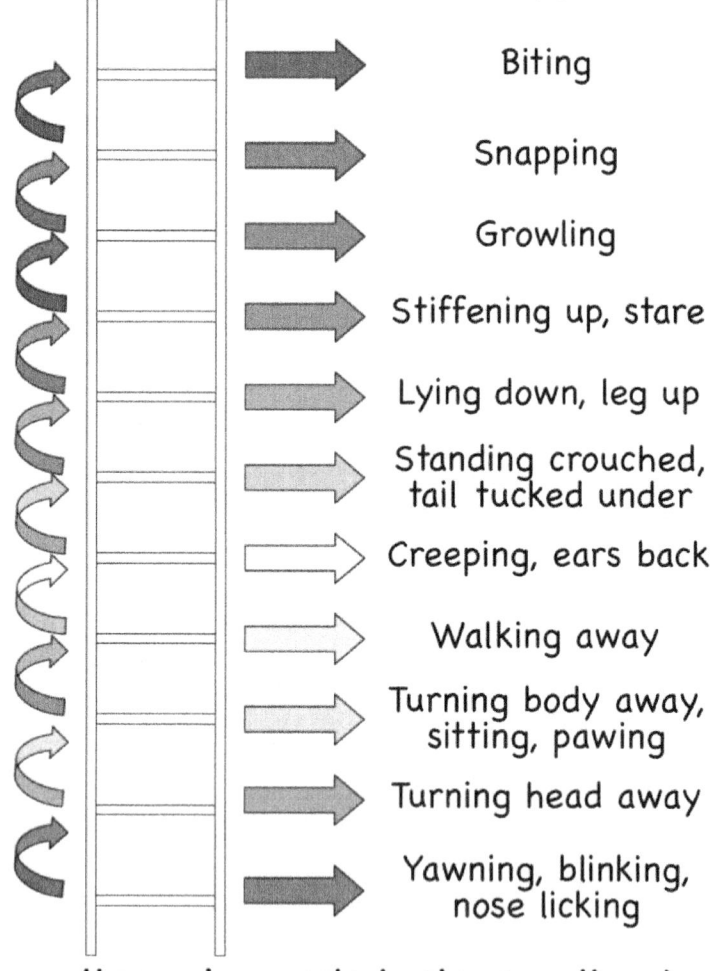

- Biting
- Snapping
- Growling
- Stiffening up, stare
- Lying down, leg up
- Standing crouched, tail tucked under
- Creeping, ears back
- Walking away
- Turning body away, sitting, pawing
- Turning head away
- Yawning, blinking, nose licking

How a dog reacts to stress or threat

©Kendal Shepherd 2004

Torso And Hair

When a dog is aroused, whether, through stress or happy excitement, its body can look very tense. Muscles can stand out – unless you have a very hairy or chubby dog – and you can see their hackles. This is the hair that runs from their neck and along the top of their back, and it can stand up on end. Seeing hackles does not necessarily mean aggression or worry, as it can also be seen when dogs are super happy and playing. It's the arousal hormones kicking in. For some dogs, you can see their pattern of hair (less obvious on curly-haired breeds) so any changes in the pattern of how their hair lies can be an indicator of pain so keep a close eye on whether the hair pattern or colour changes and check in with your vet if you are concerned.

Hackles on a dog

Freeze

When a dog first sees another dog (or human/animal) in the distance, it can freeze on the spot. This is natural and gives them time to assess whether there is danger or not ahead. This freeze makes their body tense and can last a split second. If it goes on for a few seconds or longer, then be alert to both your dog and whatever is approaching. Most often, the freeze is followed by either happy/friendly gestures or stressed/worried gestures.

Distribution Of Weight

Normally your dog will balance equally on all four paws (assuming no injury or medical issues). When your dog leans back, quite often it is because they are concerned, and trying to move away. This often happens if another dog approaches, or more commonly when a human stranger looms overhead with their hand outstretched aiming for their head. This can be intimidating for your dog so be their guardian and keep strangers away – your dog is not public property. Most dogs do not like hands on their heads anyway.

The opposite is your dog leaning forwards. This is often accompanied by lunging and barking and can be a key sign of frustration. Maybe your dog just wants to get to see/meet something nearby. Or they want to go and play but you are holding back on their lead. It can be that your dog is lunging and barking because they want to shout to keep the other dog away – they do not want them to approach. Looking out for any other stress signs may help you decide which it is, but in either case, it is useful to teach your dog to disengage and focus back on you.

Dogs will also move sideways. They may start by turning their head away, and sometimes still keep their eye on you so you see the whites of their eyes – think the spooky pictures with moving eyes in *Scooby Doo* cartoons! But this is not comedy, your dog is seriously worried and trying to say so. Leaning away with their whole body is even stronger communication. I see this so often in photos with children. Dogs do not like to be hugged tight. They prefer an escape route so they can remove themselves from uncomfortable situations.

Changes in balance of dogs

weight forward - alert

leaning back with paw lift

full body lean back

Leaning back

Cowering

Your dog will do this to make themselves appear smaller when they are super anxious. Their bodies will sink low so their shoulders protrude upwards, their head will be lowered, their tail is most often tucked down, and they may slink along. Help your dog in this situation by understanding when they do this and intervene if you can.

Dogs cowering in fear

Conversely, you may see this if you have a true hunter, and they are stalking some prey. But here, their tail will often be alert, pointing out, and they are using stealth to close a gap on the unsuspecting bird. And hopefully, the bird sees in advance and can fly away out of reach. It's all about context.

This is a dog doing what it was bred to do—stalking and working!

Lying On Their Backs

Put into context, during play a dog may lie on their back and their body is soft. The tail is often outstretched and they appear to be smiling – their jaw is relaxed and the eyes are almond-shaped. They may twist their body so they look curved, and their paws are wide away from their torso.

Quite often, if a dog is very anxious about another dog approaching, they may roll onto their back and be mistakenly called submissive. The dog is tense, its tail is often tucked up under between its legs hiding its genitals, and its paws can be covering its chest. They may even be trying to 'bat' the other dog away. Their mouth can be clamped shut and they are most certainly not being submissive but scared about the encounter. If you know your dog does this, then instead of creating a situation to escalate where your dog is exceptionally worried, instead interrupt the approaching dog by chatting, cueing a 'sit', or anything really to give your dog a chance to move away where they will feel safer.

Relaxed and happy

Lying down differences

Stressed and anxious

Tail

The tail is a really important communication tool, but not every dog has one, or one that is easily visible from a distance. I will go through what some of the expressions mean but do remember that some breeds carry their tails differently so what may mean scared to your dog, could mean relaxed to another. Yes, it's a minefield but some knowledge is really helpful here.

Your starting point is your dog's normal relaxed tail position. Not all dogs can do the full range of movements either, so when you look at the tail you must look at the whole dog as well. The tail only gives us a small part of the picture.

If alert and unsure, the tail may bolt further upright and be still, commonly seen during the initial freeze at the sight of something. To show that they don't mean any harm, the tail may wag from side to side, and even a fast wag motion. Imagine waving a white flag of peace to oncoming strangers and you won't be too far from the truth. Watch the whole body and the reaction to the other dog that is approaching.

If your dog continues to be worried and doesn't want the other dog to approach, it will often lower its tail and tuck it very close to its body, or curl it under between its legs. Dogs get information about each other from their 'pheromone farts' and by covering their bottoms they are reducing the amount of fart leakage from them. Remember though that for some dogs like Whippets and Salukis, this is their normal tail carriage. Their tails almost disappear under their belly.

Understanding Your Dog By Their Body Language

Tail positions that are not relaxed for these dogs

Alert

Anxious, tail tucked under

If the approaching dog is socially immature or not savvy in communication, they may not see that this is a sign to say 'keep your distance'. Help your dog. If the other one continues to get close, your dog may sit down to cover their bottom even more. Is this screaming not working? Then they may lie down on their backs with their tail tucked under.

Teach your dog to trust you by intervening, or asking the other owner to call their dog away before they get too close. But is it your teenage hooligan dog doing the approaching? Then start reading the body language of the other dog and call your pup, or put them on a lead. It is prudent to teach your dog that it is okay to not go up to every other dog. It's a good skill to learn and important to make sure encounters are safe and appropriate. It may not be right to allow your pup to jump on a dog that is frail, small, on a lead, needs space, or is grumpy or injured. Or in car parks and other dangerous places.

What can be fun to see is when your dog is soooo happy, its tail makes its rear end sway, and the tail can even spin like a helicopter. Just laugh at this, it is beautiful to watch.

Bowing

You may have seen your dog lower their chest but keep its butts in the air – this can be a fantastic stretch after waking up, or the bow can be used when communicating with other dogs. The main reason in play is to get the other dog to move – it creates space, and even a chase game as the other dog moves back. Or they come together to wrestle and pin each other down – playfully hopefully. But the way it becomes play is if the other dog is willing to engage. I have often seen one dog repeatedly do this to another, but the second dog is turning their heads, looking away, keeping still and all the other signs to say they are not interested. This means the first dog is struggling to read and understand other dogs' communication which is common with young dogs. Help your teenager, and the other dog, by getting your dog's focus and calling them away to have a game with you instead.

Bow – used mostly in play between dogs

Head and Face

So much communication between dogs happens with their faces, and with the breeding of changes to the face and head, sometimes this can be hard for your dog to interpret.

Many aspects make this difficult – flat faces, bulging round eyes, lack of ears, black eyes on black faces, and curly, fluffy hair hiding many signals. The more you can learn to help your dog, the better things will be.

Furrowed Brow

Admittedly, this one cannot be seen on any fluffy dog – my dog Reba included. And there are some dogs with permanent furrows – Bulldogs or Shar-Peis. But on smoother-coated dogs, this is certainly a sign that they are worried.

Furrowed brow

Mouth And Tongue

Generally, the mouth is relaxed, and when out on walks, your dog's lower jaw may be lower making the dog smile a bit. When they spot something they are unsure of, their mouth can clamp shut and on the smooth-coated dogs (i.e. ones without massive hairy beards) you can see dimples as they pull their mouths back towards their ears. If they are worried, you will also see the 'freeze' and tension in their bodies, and the tail position may change. You need to look at the whole dog, not just one sign.

Mouth clamped closed

Dogs may hold their mouths wide and even yawn. Now, if they have just woken up or are about to go to bed, of course, a yawn is quite natural, and often have a good old stretch bow with it. If they are anxious, they may yawn when you are not expecting them to.

Yawn – sometimes dogs will cover their teeth carefully

A very common early anxiety sign is licking their noses – a quick flick. This is not just when wiping food off their noses, but at other times. Maybe you are preparing to leave the house when they don't like being home alone, or they encounter a strange noise or dog when out and about. The nose lick is quite easy to see, even on black curly dogs. One nose lick is nothing to worry about but be warned, if your dog continues to feel uncomfortable and shows other signs then absolutely stop what you were doing, move away, or do something else to help your dog.

Nose licking

Dogs can curl their lips up and show their teeth. This can be on one side like an Elvis pose, or they will lift their front lip and make a wrinkled nose. This one is a serious warning and it is your responsibility to listen to keep everyone safe.

Wrinkled nose, lip lifting to show teeth – not a friendly situation

Panting

Dogs struggle to regulate their temperature, so panting is important to them. This is why you should **never** use a muzzle that clamps their mouth closed. Only vets need these, and even just for very short periods. The rate of panting should be monitored – dogs will pant when they are anxious and you can often see other signs alongside this. They may yawn or gulp between pants.

Stress panting – look at the wide eyes, the ears back and raised eyebrows that are going with the panting, and the very wide mouth pulled back at the corners.

Dogs also pant when they are very hot, and their tongue tends to go flat like a spatula so that more heat evaporates. Do keep a close eye on your dog if they are panting hard, as heat stroke kills a dog quickly by multi-organ failure. Get them out of the heat, put water over them, and call the vet.

Growling

Dogs will vocalise, and the growl can be for two main reasons. A higher-pitched growl can be heard when dogs are playing. This can be playing tug with you, or when they are wrestling with another dog. The trick to knowing if this is a 'happy' growl is by observing the body language. Are they bowing, or floppy bodies with helicopter tails?

I was once walking two cocker spaniels and they started playing beautifully. They took turns chasing, bumping into each other, stopping and shaking, starting again and they were having a ball. But...they both growled when playing. It sounded like a riot. I even had other walkers run up to me in the park wondering if I needed help separating them. If you could have turned off the volume, you would be smiling at the wonderful playtime. Their bodies were soft and wriggly, butts in the air and huge smiling faces. Both dogs growled when they played but aggression was furthest from their minds.

The other type of growl is one to be very cautious of – and never, ever tell a dog off for growling. It's your last warning before a bite. This is often a much lower pitch, guttural growl, and the body is stiff, eyes round and staring, and you want to either get out of there – or move away and stop what you were doing. If you have children, make sure they understand that this is their last chance – ideally, you have taught them the other body language, so your dog never has to resort to growling at them.

A Note About Bites

If you learn about your dog, then I hope that you never have to experience any bites. But this is your dog screaming to the other to back off. It is the last resort for many dogs, as there is a risk of injury to them, but they are at the end of their tether. Keep repeating your action? They won't start with a lick/paw lift, they have learned that only a bite works.

Remember we already learnt that adolescent dogs struggle to control their emotions. Bites can be more common at this age as they deal with their hormones, environment, the relationships of everyone around them, and more. Set your dog up for success and help them out. Supervise all and every human encounter, and be aware of other dogs too. Bites are rarely out of the blue, there has always been a history or build up and your dog has been warning you, but it's your fault to ignore these.

Eyes

Dog's eyes are normally more almond-shaped – unless your dog has been specifically bred with wide round eyes.

Dogs can squint, and if it is with a relaxed, wriggly body, then it is fairly safe to say that they are being super happy to see you and have some interaction with you. If they are squinting, leaning back, and maybe cowering a bit, then your dog is fearful and scared. What can you do to move away from the perceived danger? Be your dog's advocate and get away.

For most dogs, when they make their eyes round, they can look as if they are staring hard – and this is a seriously unhappy dog. Don't put your hand close. The body may be tense, and they may also be silent so don't assume a dog always growls before a bite. The best thing you can do is give the dog space. You can see how some dogs can be misread, as they have permanently staring eyes. Even if they are showing all friendly signs, other dogs see the stare and immediately get defensive. You need to step in to help diffuse the situation. I quite often say a loud 'hello' and wave my hand – it can break the trance and allows both dogs to read the other friendly signs.

Different eyes - worried, round, squinting with ears back - all of these dogs are anxious or scared

Ears

What do your dog's ears look like? Are they upright like beacons, or floppy like pancakes? Their hearing is phenomenal and can hear a much wider range than us mere humans. They will twist and turn, and be very expressive so they can work out the different sounds and from which direction it is coming from. Even the floppy-eared dogs can raise them – they look like a Gizmo...or Yoda – depending on what films you like to watch.

When alert, they are pinned forward, listening carefully. When they are anxious or fearful, they will often be pressed back and flatter against their heads. Have a close watch of your dog and see what positions they can get in, look at the context and learn. By observing your dog, you can learn a lot about how they feel at that moment, and that will help you manage the situation you are in at that time.

Alert with ears forward

Ears

Anxious with ears pinned back

What to look for when dogs play together

Dogs communicate a lot with each other during play, and as long as the other one is listening, then all is okay. It may seem like a fight to us, but there are key things to look for: signals between dogs, the balance of play, inhibition, self-handicapping their strength/size to smaller dogs, and inefficient movements. The best YouTube video I have seen is by Jane Sigsworth of DogKnowledge – there are two videos of Dog Dog Play... the first shows examples of good play and the second is the consent test.

Dogs develop different play styles with different dogs – my girl Reba loves to be chased more than chasing another dog, so play is not always 50/50. Her partner in crime gets her to move, then stops to watch, then ambush her when she runs past and so it repeats. Indoors, with another friend, they do more 'gentle' wrestling than anything else. Look for both stopping or copying each other – both need to listen to each other.

Good dog/dog play

Both these pairs are very good friends and know the play styles each other prefers

As we found out before, dogs are not social butterflies all their lives, and your teenage dog may not want to go up to every dog to say 'hello', let alone play, even if they have not played with another for a while. Don't force them. Let them choose. If your dog loves to run up to everyone, then it is better to teach them to ignore some dogs too. Not every dog wants a stranger barrelling up to them and jumping over them. So use your discretion, watch the body language of the other dog as well as your own, and make a judgement call as to whether it is appropriate.

If you think the play is too boisterous, or one-sided, then do the consent test. This is where you separate the dogs and release the one that you think is not happy. If they go straight back in, then they are having fun. If they do nothing or move away, then keep the other dog on a lead or separate, as the first dog is thankful for the break. Do this occasionally so that it does not lead to tears or tantrums – for dogs or humans.

And don't be a lazy owner by waiting for a stranger's dog to do your job for you – it is not the responsibility of another dog to tell your dog to go away – you need to step up and be responsible. You are only making the other dog more reactive to their space being invaded uninvited. Your dog is only learning to be a bully. If your dog is more cautious, then you also need to be their advocate and interrupt other dogs, or even tell the human that it is **not** okay to just approach and ruffle your dog's hair. Teach your dog that they can trust you.

Dogs And Children

Children find it tough to spot the subtle signs of stress in dogs, and may not realise what their actions are doing to the dog, or how the dog is feeling during the encounter. Interactions must always be supervised. If your dog is not getting heard, and the prodding, hugging and grabbing of them continues, then your dog will escalate their response, including up to bite level.

Dogs are not cuddly toys, and you need both your dog and children to be safe at all times.

Look at the following photos of dogs and children, and can you see any of the stress signs that have been mentioned above? Do these dogs look happy to you? Or do they look like they want to get out of there?

What signs can you spot in all of these pics that show the dog is not happy...?

Dogs do not like to be hugged, restrained or sat on......

Now, look at how your family is interacting with your dog. What do you see your dog doing? Just because you are enjoying the hug/cuddle, doesn't mean your dog is.

Talking Dog

By now, you should have a better understanding of your dog and how they communicate. Look at the whole dog, the context of the situation and the environment they are in at the time.

Ignore at your peril!

But by learning to speak dog, your bond and relationship will grow stronger, and we learned in Chapter 1 how important that is to survive the adolescence phase.

4

CREATING CALM

Is your adolescent dog constantly on the go?

Always demanding attention?

Ever wanted them to just settle and give you a few minutes of peace?

This is a skill that needs to be taught, but there are other factors to consider too.

Dogs do not automatically know that they have an 'off' switch, and some busy dogs find it hard to switch off and learn to relax. Others just want your focus and attention all the time, or they will go and entertain themselves, normally in your rubbish bin or chewing the children's toys. In this chapter, I will take you through a few ways to help your dog become calmer at home.

First, we need to understand their routine and if there are aspects of it that are making them more hyperactive. In Chapter 1, I talked about the myriad of hormones that affect the transition from puppy to adulthood, but there are plenty more of them that affect their behaviour, both indoors and outside.

Serotonin is the 'happy' hormone and promotes bonding, calm and just loving life. With this, they find they can cope better in different environments, and it helps your dog to be more resilient with whatever is happening around them.

Cortisol is the hormone that is released when they are stressed. This can be if they are super hyper-excited, have been rushing around lots (for example at a large daycare centre) or it can be coursing through them if they are anxious, worried or fearful. It's a survival hormone, but too much of it can be negative for your dog and it affects their general brain chemistry as well as their learning capability.

The Stress Bucket

Imagine your dog has a bucket. Each dog's bucket can be a different size – nothing to do with their actual body size but their ability to cope. Everything that happens that releases cortisol fills that bucket. Maybe it's not even empty from the day before, as cortisol can take many days to reduce down. Each exciting encounter, each scary-looking dog, every bang heard, and even unpleasant smells releases more cortisol into their bucket. Quite quickly, this bucket can overflow. It may not be the loudest or scariest thing that tips it over, but a build-up of everything. For example, your dog may not like a black dog, a lorry noise, and kids shouting. If one thing happens, then that can be coped with, but if all three happened in quick succession, then there is not enough time for your dog to process and so they overreact to the kids shouting, only because they were already stressed from the lorry and black dog.

But, their bucket has holes. The number and size of holes can be increased so that the level of the bucket doesn't reach the top. Increasing the leaks can build resilience and confidence in your dog, and improve training as they are in a better position to listen, and cope.

If your dog has a crazy or scary day, then there is nothing wrong with *not* walking them the next day. Let their hormones settle, and the bucket empty. Having a wonderful 'duvet day' with you will be good for both of you, as you may have felt anxious or worried at an encounter too. Playing indoor games, or training tricks will keep their brains active, and a sniffing search around your home and garden will tire them out mentally. Running around just increases the hormones and fills the bucket, but sniffing and puzzles will empty it.

If they're constantly on the go, the brain is flooded with hormones that make them keep going and it's not healthy long-term. Teaching them to relax and settle is important and having this built into their routine will help both of you.

Diet

Making sure your dog has a nutritious diet has an impact on how they behave. Giving your dog the best balanced food that meets their nutritional needs can impact their ability to be calm. Having too much junk food that does not satisfy them can lead to hyperactivity. 'You are what you eat' applies to dogs too.

Self-Settling—Chews

These can be exceptionally useful and help your dog. Licking and chewing release happy hormones and can soothe your dog. The sensation on their tongues, along with brain work for the puzzle, and the dexterity of their limbs to hold the puzzle feeder or chew can be great for settling them.

Chewing is a naturally calming activity and helps your dog de-stress. Perfect for emptying the bucket. It gives them something challenging to do that they find enriching. It keeps their mouths occupied and they will bark less when you are busy, and gives them a job while visitors are there so they are less likely to jump up on them. Longer-lasting healthy chews also clean their teeth and help the gums stay healthy. Perfect.

Lick mats are very handy (and great if you are travelling). Just spread some plain cream cheese, natural yoghurt, puree veg or fruit (no toxic onion-type foods!) onto the mat and supervise them. For more challenging feeder toys, Kongs are good but can be frustrating for dogs to reach the end, so I much prefer and recommend the West Paw Toppls. These have a wider opening so are suitable for flat-faced or larger muzzled breeds too. Fill with favourite foods mixed up – and build up to freezing them to make them last longer. I have a blog post about using these feeder toys on my website as well as some recipe ideas.

Long-lasting chews are even better – again supervise your dog so they don't struggle or choke on the small remnants. Deer or Elk antlers last for ages, but I also love giving natural chews. Firm favourites for Reba are rabbit ears, salmon skin twists, and ostrich. All of these are lower fat so I can maintain her weight easily. Pork can be fatty, so do check your dog can tolerate these.

With bones, be very careful that they cannot splinter – so no cooked or weight-bearing bones. My girl has an ostrich bone and it is almost as big as her. There are some great suppliers and I have some links at the end of the book.

Whatever you do, avoid anything 'hide' or 'rawhide'. These are just chemically treated skins glued together and can be very dangerous to your dog – they cannot be broken down or digested, and can cause a lethal blockage in their gut. The only place they belong is in the bin.

Rest And Sleep

The most important aspect for your dog to be calmer and more focused is to ensure they have good quality rest and sleep. It is common for many dogs to need as much as sixteen hours or more a day of quality rest and sleep.

Make sure your dog has access to several areas to rest that are out of the main walkway of your home. Depending on the temperature and their coat type, they may need a warm soft bed or prefer a cooler surface. Provide a suitable environment to promote calmness in your dog.

Dogs are crepuscular which means they are more active in the mornings and early evenings – just when we are ready to settle down with our feet up. Their natural body clock is just different to ours, so your adolescent dog cannot help but bother you at the same time your favourite TV show is on.

We sleep for a good eight hours during the night, but our dogs have a shorter sleep cycle that repeats often. This can explain why you may hear them padding around during the night. They also have the amazing ability to be fast asleep one minute, and leaping around with excitement the next whereas we humans take a bit longer, and probably coffee, to be that active that quickly.

Making sure your dog actively goes to their bed to rest is your job. Overtired dogs will not take themselves off to bed, but you need to encourage them to their quiet spot, give them a chew or lick mat, and let them settle.

Going to their bed should never be a punishment. If they are getting overtired, they will be more cranky and this can show in being more mouthy, jumpy, barky, pestering or just being even more cheeky. There is no point in trying to tell them off, it won't work. Just encourage them to their area, leave a tasty Toppl or chew, and let them settle themselves. Next time, learn their body language signs, make a note of what was happening in their day to lead up to the problem time, and pre-empt by preparing their puzzle feeder or chew on their bed and encourage them there earlier before they cause chaos.

Here are two exercises you can try to build up a calmer time for your dog and encourage them to settle on their beds.

Rewarding nothing

Just this! Instead of always doing something, moving or anything active, and rewarding them for listening to your cues, we are going to change this up.

When your dog is doing nothing – reward them. What gets rewarded gets repeated, so if you see your dog choosing to settle, praise them. Whisper 'good dog' so they don't suddenly get excited, and they won't always need a treat either. I used to whisper the word 'settle' and then followed it with 'good' or if my dog was super lucky, I would throw a treat at her. But if your dog is a foodie like mine, they may break the settle and perk up at the thought of more food coming their way. In rewarding settling down, verbal praise is often enough. Oh, you can smile at them too.

Magic Mat

I **love** this game! It's the cornerstone of so many solutions to the challenges you may have. It gives your dog permission to relax, it gives them a focal point too.

Have you imagined taking your teenage dog out and about with you?

Does your image involve them lying by your feet in a café? Or under the table in a pub?

Maybe they settle by your side while you visit a friend, and do not charge around with the potential to damage their ornaments.

Then you need the Magic Mat.

It takes time to build a love for it, so don't rush this one.

All you need is a towel and lots of treats.

I use a towel as it is so portable. I can put it over her normal bed, I can place it next to me on the sofa – yes, there is nothing wrong with your dog on the sofa if you want them to, it doesn't make them 'dominant' (total myth and untruth) or take over your life (well, they do that last bit but we want them to). I can also place the towel on the floor next to the table in the pub/café/restaurant and I can reposition it around the home if I need my dog to settle in different places. And a towel is very washable.

Phase 1

Start indoors, where there are the fewest distractions.

1. Place the towel on the floor and be ready with the treats. As soon as your dog looks at the towel, throw a treat onto it.
2. If your dog moves closer, throw another treat, and for every movement towards the towel.

3. If they put any body part on the towel – a hair, a nail, a whisker, or even better a paw – drop a few treats one at a time in quick succession.
4. The aim now is to drop treats from above their heads while they are looking down and eating the previous treat. This encourages them to keep their noses low and not sit and beg at you.
5. If they move away, stop and wait.
6. If they move back to the mat, throw treats again.
7. Next time, only treat if they have 2 paws on. Anything less doesn't get rewarded.
8. Yes, you guessed it – now 3 paws! And then 4.
9. Are they starting to hang around on the mat? Fantastic. You can test this by throwing one treat away from the towel. They should move off it to get the food…but how quickly do they return to it? Say and do nothing, just let them work it out.
10. Slow down the treats to one every few seconds, and see if they park their bottom on it. If they move into a sit position – yippee! Now you will only drop treats if they sit.
11. Move to another position around the mat – don't always treat from the same side.
12. In time, they may even lie down on the mat. This is excellent progress.

Keep your sessions to a few minutes, or a set number of treats, then take a break. Short training sessions are more productive than spending ages and ages doing the same thing. That just gets boring and frustrating.

If you are taking a break, lift the mat away. You don't want it lying around without any rewards. It will lose its magic.

To keep your dog on the mat longer, slow down the rate of dropping treats, and then place down a stuffed feeder toy or chew.

Phase 2

Time to slowly increase distractions by now placing the mat in a different location in the home. You may have to go through each of the steps in Phase 1 and build the love again.

Then take your mat outside into your garden – this is harder for your dog as there are more smells, more movement and more distractions there.

Next, go to your local coffee shop avoiding the busiest times, and maybe just sit outside for a few minutes and do some mat training. Keep hold of the lead for safety. You will need to build up time slowly to the point where you can relax and drink a coffee, and build up even more time if you plan to eat too.

Now, pub visits. The first time they go, it is unlikely they will settle for anywhere near long enough for you to enjoy a drink or even a meal, so build up the time there slowly.

If your dog is struggling, then it is too challenging for them. Be prepared to leave and get your dog to a quieter place to relax again. And then go back a step or two and build up to that level of distraction again – is there a way to make it easier for them? Maybe inside a pub on a busy weekend is too overwhelming, so what about outside at a quieter time of the week first?

Your adolescent dog may struggle to sit quietly for several hours while you enjoy a Sunday roast and a read of the paper, so think about what they can manage, and can you compromise? That way you will both be happy.

If you haven't done any Magic Mat for a while, don't assume your teenage dog will automatically remember it. Their brains are like jelly while they reform the connections, so go back to the beginning and get them loving it again, let the magic work.

Creating Calm

Mat training – sometimes it may not go to plan but the aim is for a settle!

Teaching your dog to be calm is a skill, and some breeds such as spaniels find this hard so go with your dog's ability, and go at their pace when they are learning the mat game. Some dogs get this quickly, others take more time and encouragement. They are all individuals.

Remember, sleep and quality rest, long-lasting chews, and rewarding nothing can be essential for your dog to learn to relax at home. And your Magic Mat is a game-changer for settling when out and about.

5

BARKING

Dogs bark as a way of communicating to both us as owners and to other dogs.

Humans respond more to their barking because we have probably missed all those subtle bits of body language that dogs display when they're trying to tell us something. So it's not till they raise their voices and bark at us that we tend to listen.

Dogs are commonly expected to be quiet and react to nothing. That is a big challenge and one that can be unrealistic for many dogs. What we would like is to allow some barking to let us know what is happening, but also to be able to tell a dog when it is enough and they can go and relax. It is impossible to expect a dog to never bark. However, we don't want constant barking that can be distressing for everyone, and anyone in the vicinity who can hear it.

Why do some dogs bark more than others?

There can be many factors, and the first one to look at is what they are naturally bred to do. This will give you a clue as to how vocal your dog may be.

Quite a lot of dogs are genetically bred to bark more than others.

Hunters can either be stalking stealth types, or certainly for smaller breeds, they would see their prey, and bark wildly to make it run. Then they can chase and catch it. An example would be Dachshunds who would bark at the prey to stun it into fear down the hole where they can then grab it. These dogs are not quiet lapdogs but are very vocal as their job is to be noisy when hunting.

Maybe they are bred to be alert dogs, such as livestock guarding breeds for example Shepherds or Mountain Dogs. Their hearing is very sensitive so they can hear any threat or intruder early, and then bark to alert their presence to protect the livestock. It's a warning not only to the intruder to stay away but also to the owner so they can come out and assist. They can also bark at the livestock should one wander off, so they will bark and run around to herd it back to the main flock.

When dogs can't express these natural behaviours then they will quite often bark at what they perceive as a stray sheep. And that could be a moving car, a cyclist, or a family member that peeled off from the group to go somewhere. Barking is like them saying 'hey, you're not sticking together, you're moving away'. Their instinct would be to bark at the rogue wanderer and go and herd them back in. It's a natural thing for them to do, their job.

Humans have tapped into these abilities and encouraged aspects for certain breeds to help them work with us in various jobs. But many of these working breeds are now stay-at-home pets, without their job but all of their instincts. And living close to neighbours who may not appreciate the constant chatter (bark, howl or whatever your dog does) disturbing their peace.

Knowing what your dog was bred to do, and then finding them alternative activities that appease this part of their natural behaviour will help them feel more satisfied and can help with the barking. For example, with gundogs, hide favourite toys for them to search and retrieve, or tasty food to find and eat. It may not be appropriate to let your herding dog into a field of sheep, so this is also where you can teach them how to cope with what can be against their instinct and manage the barking.

Coping with excessive barking

To work out what you can do about excessive barking, you first need to find out why your dog is barking or the situations that set them off. They can vocalise for many reasons, and by finding the trigger, you can then apply a solution that will help your dog to understand when they can shout and when to be quiet and to know that you will also help them out of a sticky spot. The barking can sound different to each reason, so listen to your dog and get to know the volume, frequency and pitch of their barks.

There's no point in just telling them to 'shut up', 'be quiet' or keep repeating 'no, no, no'. They don't understand the meaning behind our language or words. All they respond to is how you look and your tone of voice, and maybe look scary to them with our angry faces. Or your talking/shouting only makes you join in the conversation where neither side understands the other and make the other one shout louder to be heard. Oops. Finding out why, and then what you can do will help both of you.

I will now go through some common reasons and what you can do to help.

Excitement Barking

Frequently during play, dogs will bark excitedly. It can be quite a high-pitched bark and often in a regular pattern. This may not be a problem when out on a walk with good dog/dog play but can become annoying if your dog is pumped full of adrenaline and you have come home and need it to be quieter.

Maybe change their activities outside to have less 'adrenaline junkie' high-pace physicality, but include longer sniffing time before you get home. Sniffing engages the thinking part of the brain, and can lower arousal hormones. Rapid sniffing also lowers their heart rate, so is an excellent way to cool down your dog after exertion. Scent discrimination takes up nearly 40% of their brain too, so they will be tired as well. By changing your habits just a bit, you may find that as you get home, your dog is calmer and happier to then go and snooze rather than be rowdy and noisy, high on hormones.

Attention Barking

This can be barking because they need something or a learnt behaviour.

1 - Start with ruling out any welfare needs.

This means checking if they are hungry and close to mealtime. If there is a while to go yet, consider a small chew or a few low-calorie treats to keep the tummy rumbles at bay. Dogs have a more acidic stomach than us, and when it is empty, it can make them nauseous and sick. Just a small biscuit will keep the stomach happy, and your dog will feel better for it too.

Maybe your dog needs to go out to the toilet. By now, you will have a good idea of how often your dog needs to wee, but it may be a day that they are not feeling as perky, so still need to go out at other times. To help with getting them to the toilet quicker, I have a special word (Go Biz) that I used when my girl was a puppy every time she squatted. Now I can say this to get her to go quickly and not be so distracted by the garden. No treats, her reward is the relief and the opportunity to go sniffing if she wants to afterwards. If they are easily distracted in the garden, keep your dog on a lead in their specified area until they have been, and then let them off the lead for a run or sniff.

2 - Next, look at their emotional needs.

Are they bored? Dogs can get quite barky if they are frustrated and cannot find something to do. There is a danger they will create their own entertainment by rummaging in bins or chewing on your sofa cushions. Teaching them to settle and giving them a long-lasting chew will help you here. Go to Chapter 4 for ideas on how to get your dog to settle. Dogs get a dopamine hormone hit when they forage and search, so utilise treat dispensing toys to break that boredom.

If they won't settle, maybe they need more enrichment by a walk. It doesn't have to be a long run, as using their brains uses more calories. Visiting places where there are lots of smells is even better to satisfy your dog. They are built to smell first, and that is how they establish their world. Drop treats into long grass or piles of leaves to encourage their noses to go down. If your dog has restricted exercise, then consider gathering up leaves, grass and twigs and placing them on a tray indoors – then your dog can still get the 'local news' without leaving home. Making sure your dog is physically and mentally satiated will be much better for all of you when you need them to relax and not bark.

3 - Has your dog learnt to bark at you for attention?

Very often, when dogs first bark at us, our instinct is to react. We may look, talk, touch or play with the dog to stop them from barking. However, even by eye contact or saying anything, this can be a reward to your dog as they have you interacting with them. Bingo. Is this something that is happening to you?

Think about the situations where your dog may be barking at you for attention. What is the cycle? Have you just stopped the tug game but they want more? Have you just stopped tickling their belly? They bark, so you carry on where you left off.

We are not the only ones that train here, dogs train us to do behaviours on their cues too.

I see a lot of dogs that bark and become obsessed with balls and sticks when out on walks. Chasing is massive for every hunter. It gives an adrenaline spike. The ball or stick becomes more important than us, which is why I personally never take them out on walks with me. I need my dog to listen to me instead of only responding if I carry a ball.

When we stop walking, your dog may bark at you. If you are trying to have a conversation then to stop the dog barking, you throw a ball (remember, sticks can be dangerous and hurt their mouths so these are not recommended). The dog chases the ball, has super fun, and may even bring the ball back to you. They step back a few paces and bark at you again. You pick up the ball and throw it. Your dog has learnt that if it barks loudly, you play the game by throwing the ball for them. You are also rewarding them for keeping away from you which is not helpful for any recall training. I have seen where the owner then got a puppy and guess what happened…if it barks, you throw a ball for them to chase. They now have two very loud barking dogs on the walk that never stopped until they got home.

You have inadvertently taught your dog to bark at you for a game.

On your next walk, think about other ways to interact with your dog. Limit the ball games to hiding the ball for them to find which is equally rewarding for them, but lower arousal. And only hide it when they are off sniffing so they cannot get that adrenaline spike. Also, it breaks the cycle of barking at you to get you to throw it.

Alert Barking

Many dogs are territorial and will alert you when strangers approach them or their home. The bark is deeper and more staccato. There may be a tiny huff before the full barking starts, or even a little growl between barks.

Often dogs will bark at people walking past, or delivery and post workers going up to your door. They naturally bark, and the person moves away. The human was continuing to walk past anyway, however, your dog didn't know this. In your dog's mind, they shouted at them when they got close and made the human move. So next time, they reckon that to make them move again, they will bark as it did the trick last time. Barking at humans makes them move away from them.

Now, if someone loiters on your doorstep as you have to sign for something, your dog is wondering why their initial bark didn't work so more than likely will bark longer and harder. And guess what, the postal person turns to go, and now louder barks happen each time as that is now working better.

It creates a cycle and the worst thing we can do is join in with the raised emotions by shouting at our dog to be quiet. You both get louder and louder.

Instead, think about how you can manage the situation. If your dog is an avid window watcher but has a habit of barking at everyone, use netting or stick-on frosted film on the lower part of the window so the view is obscured. Each time they go to the window but then turn and move away, mark and reward for doing so. Keep at this. It can take time to break a habit, but perseverance and consistency is the key.

If they are triggered by noise, then have a radio on, or maybe white/brown/grey noise that muffles exterior sounds. If you are expecting a delivery and you get to see them approach, start feeding your dog treats so that they associate the approaching person with good stuff, and will in future be less likely to bark at them. Instead, they will start to look forward to the post-person as that means tasty treats.

If they are noisy in the garden, then it is difficult to control neighbours and wildlife, but can you screen off gaps in fences with planters or fencing? Rather than leave your dog to their own devices, go out with them so you can be ready to distract them ideally before they start barking, or with your 'enough' cue and reward them on the spot for stopping barking. Find out what is in the environment to cause them to bark.

Doorbells and doorknocks

Very similar to the alert barking, this can be triggered by the noise of the doorbell and/or the sight of someone walking past. If you think about how we react, as soon as the doorbell goes we jump up and rush to the door. Our dogs have just been copying us. However, do we expect them to ignore the doorbell? At the door there can be post, visitors, or the exit point to wonderful walks.

Teaching your dog an 'Enough' cue will help.

<u>Enough</u>

Be ready with tasty chicken (or similar) and practice when there is no one coming to your home. You will first pretend, teach your dog what you want them to do, and build up to real people.

Step 1

While staying inside, knock on your door and let your dog bark a few times – we all like the alert, to begin with. Then hold the chicken by their nose and slowly move it away and let the dog's nose follow the chicken. Initially, this will be to turn their heads away from the door. Feed them.

Repeat this a few times. Then introduce your 'Enough' cue just before you feed them. By this point, they probably will have stopped barking to take the food.

Now be one step away from the door and repeat.

Step 2

Do the above but without the chicken by their nose. Knock on the inside of the door, and after a bark, say 'enough' and as soon as your dog has turned their head and moved away a little bit from the door, bring out the treat and feed them.

You can use the doorbell noise by recording it and playing it on your phone, or if you have one you can just press the receiver unit rather than having to reach outside to press the button.

Step 3

Keep building this up with you further away from the door, and instead of using food, interact and praise your dog in other ways such as a game or some trick moves as the reward.

Step 4

Now get some friends involved.

Have them ring the bell/knock on the door when you send a text, while you work on your 'enough' cue inside. You won't be opening the door as you want your dog to be quiet and calmer first.

When your dog is doing great, then you can start opening the door.

Safety point—your dog is likely to be excited at seeing a visitor, so use a stairgate, or put them on a lead so they cannot rush out of the door into the road when you open it.

Step 5

Get your dog to go to their bed by using the doorbell noise as the cue. If they already understand the cue 'bed' then play the doorbell noise, ask them to go to bed – walk with them with a treat, to begin with, then reward and praise them. In time, they will learn to go to the bed on the doorbell rather than you also needing to guide them.

Step 6

Some dogs can still bark again so after giving the 'enough' cue, get them to retrieve a favourite toy. Most dogs cannot bark with a stuffed toy in their mouths.

The 'enough' cue can work in other situations too.

My girl will bark at birds in the garden so I have just waited for her to stop, said 'enough', dropped a treat and walked back indoors. Soon I could interrupt her barking with a quietly spoken 'enough' and she will stop and walk into the house. Rewards are mostly praise, but occasionally she will have a surprise food treat, which makes it worth her while to keep responding to me.

Once learnt, you can try this out and about too. It won't work every time or in every situation though.

Frustration/Fear Barking

This barking is commonly directed at other dogs or people when out and about. The difference is their body language. What are they doing at the time of barking?

A scared dog may cower, have its tail low, its ears back and the other stress signs talked about in Chapter 3. They will be barking to try and keep the other dog (or human) away from them, to keep the space. In this situation, move away from the trigger, let your dog have more space and get in touch with a Clinical Animal Behaviourist (CAB). I only will refer to a CAB as they are fully regulated, and will not make your dog worse or use aversive methods that can escalate the behaviour. Sadly, the industry is mostly unregulated so anyone can pretend they can 'fix' a dog. I will provide you with where to go for professional help at the end of the book.

Alternatively, your dog could be frustrated. They want to go over and say 'hello' but you are holding them back on the lead. Dogs that have not been socialised well, or have confidence issues can bark with frustration as they are not sure what else to do. It may not be appropriate to allow your dog to meet the other one.

One way to help your dog is to build focus and confidence in the proximity of other dogs. This means that they don't get to run over and jump on the other dog every time, as that is bad manners. Instead, find other dogs who are older, and more socially savvy, and while keeping space between them, scatter food at your feet for them to find, guide them to put their paws on objects or tree stumps (dog parkour) or teach them some snazzy tricks. They learn to focus on you as you are engaging with them and they also learn that other dogs nearby are fun without having to knock them over and wrestle them.

If you need to walk past other dogs and your dog is barking out of frustration, then talk to your dog calmly, distract them, and reward them for any slight turn away from the trigger. Keeping your anxiety and tension low is key.

Read your dog's body language and if it is safe to do so, with the other owner's knowledge, just follow their dog, to begin with. Your dog will smell and absorb all the information about the other without needing to get up close and personal.

Often this is enough for your dog to calm down and not bark at the other one. They just wanted to find out who they were.

Distress Barking

As dogs have been bred to be with us, then many do not cope when alone. Separation Anxiety is a common problem, but many owners are not aware as it happens when they are out of the house. It may not be constant noise, but higher-pitched barking and crying with pauses between the barks. They are not being naughty but having panic attacks at being home alone.

Leaving them to cry it out has been proven time and again to fail. They don't learn to 'get over it' as they are in a state of fear, a phobic reaction. Having the stress hormones flooding their brains repeatedly, and then always being hyper-alert to you moving in case you disappear on them is unhealthy both physically and mentally. They are unable to relax at home and this can cause other health issues.

Separation Anxiety can be helped, but it is a long process of slow, gradual exposure. Many of my clients start by going to touch the door, as their dogs are distressed even by the owners leaving the room.

Finally

All the exercises are progressed at your dog's pace for all of these situations, and if you carefully train your dog to emotionally cope, and provide suitable alternative things to do or behaviours, then the results will be longer lasting.

Keeping calm and consistent will give confidence to your dog, but be mindful of how often you are exposing them to the things that make them bark and react. While you are working on the solutions, do your best to change your routine and avoid the triggers as much as you can. Then slowly introduce them again such as planned visitors or ball games.

For example, with Separation Anxiety, if the dog is scared of being home alone, then we suspend absences away from the dog and that means getting in a lot of help, sitters and day care days so that your dog doesn't have to keep experiencing the fear because otherwise your training is just not going to work very well.

Similarly, if your dog is nervous and barking at other dogs then a day care centre is not going to be great because you keep exposing your dog to too much of the scary thing which is overwhelming for them.

And maybe you need to adjust where you walk, the times of walk or even stop walking your dog as much. Instead do brain work such as training new moves, find it scent games or confidence building by exploring new objects

We don't want them to lose their voices and be silent forever, but continuous or excessive barking can be a nuisance. When does your dog bark, and when is it a problem for you?

6

JUMPING UP

Dogs will jump up on humans for many reasons and it's not always welcomed. Especially if your cute small puppy is now a large-looking dog who can reach high up. Not everyone likes muddy paw prints all over them. Dogs jumping up can be scary and intimidating. You may know that your dog is friendly, but other people don't.

Why Do Dogs Jump Up?

There can be many reasons for this, but mostly it is a natural dog behaviour. Puppies would jump up at their mum's faces to get attention or to make them lie down so they can feed.

Jumping Up

They can jump up when super excited, or they are scared and need reassurance. Or maybe they are bored and just want your attention. Maybe you are holding something good that they want to investigate.

Dogs go to other dogs' faces to get information about the other one, and so they aim to sniff our faces too as a way of greeting. As we stand up, they have to jump to try and reach our heads.

If your adolescent dog is still jumping up a lot, then have they been taught to keep their paws on the floor, or is someone still encouraging it by giving them attention?

When puppies are very small, jumping up is not such a problem as they are then easier to reach to stroke, and they are unlikely to knock you over. But each time they jump up at you, and you give any attention, or a visitor does, then that is rewarding for them so they will try it again and again.

You learnt that any attention can be rewarding, so looking at them, touching them, and talking to them can all be wonderful for your dog. Every time they leap you look, maybe shout 'no' or 'down' or even push them down but you are not telling them off, and they are not being stubborn, instead, you are rewarding them for jumping up.

I have often seen clients that have just said 'down' when the dog is jumping up. Remember that dogs learn by associations, and they now associate the word 'down' with a leap up. The picture in your mind may look very different, but have you taught your dog what it is you wanted them to do? Do a quick test. With your dog focused on you, say your down/off/no cue. What do they do? Maybe they just do this to visitors so try then. If they bounce up as you say it, then there is your answer – down means jump.

How to manage the jumping up

If you have been saying 'down' to no avail, then stop using this word. It has become poisoned as it means the total opposite to your dog.

Have a serious talk with all family members, and find out if anyone is still inadvertently rewarding the jumping up. Maybe the dog jumps up as they come home and your family member gives the dog a good stroke or scratch in return. Or could it be visitors that smile and stroke the dog while its paws are off the floor? This is not a time for accusations, but for education. To break the habit for the dog, everyone needs to be on board and consistent. Ban visitors for a while if they won't follow your instructions.

When you or a visitor arrives through the door, have your dog behind a stairgate and keep everyone separated until the dog is calmer. They cannot listen to your cues when they are excited, the brain cannot focus during the adrenaline rush they are experiencing. Management is key so if you do not have a stairgate barrier, then have your dog on a lead and keep them at a distance so they cannot touch or jump on your guest. Do this when outside of your home too, if the dog can keep accessing people to jump up on, they won't learn the new routine but keep to the old habit.

Look at when your dog is jumping up, and then you can work out why. Are they overtired or over-excited? If so, spot the early signs and encourage them to their bed with a chew instead, or maybe end that tug game a bit earlier. Be prepared for visitors, or if you know they will jump up at you first thing in the morning (assuming they are not sleeping in the same room as you, otherwise they won't have missed you if they have been in your bedroom all night).

Teaching them to not jump up

To begin with, stop giving attention to them when they do. Slightly turn your back, twist or move away. No words, no knees or hands pushing them but stand still. If your dog is being persistent, move away and to the other side of a stairgate or door. Your dog may try harder at first as they are not getting the attention they are used to, so keep your nerve and be consistent.

This will not work by itself, as you now need to actively teach what they are supposed to do instead. There are a few options here, so try some or all – whatever works for your dog and you.

<u>Rewarding paws on the floor.</u>

You can use your marker word or clicker for this one, followed by treats. If you can, try and capture the moment your dog has paws on the floor before they are close enough to jump up on you. Click and give a treat. If they have already taken a leap, turn slightly, and wait for their 4 paws to touch the floor. Try and count to 1 before you click and treat, so you are making sure their paws have been on the floor for a second, and you are not marking the motion of landing.

If they can do this, then count to 2 seconds of paws connected to the ground before marking and rewarding.

Build in a new cue just before you click/mark the paws on the floor. Use something different to what you tried before. Maybe 'floor' is the cue to them now keeping paws on the floor, but use any word you like.

If your dog is looking at you with intent, but their feet are down and their tails wagging in happiness, mark and reward this before they get too excited and jump up. Pick up on any opportunity they have feet on the ground. The more you can capture this, the quicker your dog will learn that paws on the floor means they will get attention. Keep verbal praise lower key, as the more excited you sound, the more they will get crazy and jump.

If after using your clicker or marker word, your dog is leaping for the treat, then throw the treat on the floor each time. If their noses are down, they cannot jump up.

'Hello' cue

Say 'hello' and drop a treat by your feet for your dog. Repeat often, and say 'hello' with increasing amounts of happiness to replicate how you will greet someone for real. Your dog will associate 'hello' with putting their heads down to look for the dropped food, instead of jumping up at either of you as you greet the other person.

Teaching another action when meeting other humans

Having your dog respond reliably to a sit cue will help you. Some dogs do not find sitting comfortable due to their shape, or the surface they are on so a 'lie-down' or another action is equally suitable here. Just make sure it is something they are good at. If they cannot respond to that, then stillness with paws on the floor will be ideal too.

Now, have a friend stand at a distance. Start to approach them and when you are about 6 feet away, cue your dog to sit. If they struggle, turn away, and try again but have a bit more distance this time. Build up to 3 feet away and cue a sit. Your helper is keeping still and avoiding eye contact. Your dog should not be able to reach or touch them.

Next, your helper may look at your dog and say 'hello'. No more. Ask your dog to sit. Each time they do sit for you, don't forget to praise and treat your dog. Make it worth their while. If they can't respond, turn away, and try again with less interaction from your helper.

Build up the challenge with your helper being a little more animated each time ('ooh, there's a puppy' kind of level). And try different helpers.

Keep sessions short, about 5-10 goes a session as all those sits/downs/ups are tiring on their joints. As well as the brain's effort to concentrate for you and resist their impulse urges.

Visitors in your home

A handy tip is to separate your dog, let your visitor in and get settled. Put the lead on your dog and bring them into the room. Scatter pieces of food on the floor so that they can concentrate on hunting the treats and this can also calm them down enough to then be allowed to greet your guest calmly. If your dog gets too excited, encourage your dog away – try and avoid dragging them by the lead, instead hold a treat by their nose and lure them to follow the food in your hand away from your guest.

If your dog has a retrieve, then as visitors arrive, ask your dog to go and fetch a specific toy. This will give them something else to do instead of leaping on your guest.

If your dog loves their bed, will they go to their bed with visitors there? This is hard for them as they may be excited, but having a chew on their bed, or a tasty stuffed feeder toy may give them an outlet for the adrenaline and focus on food rather than the humans.

Out on walks

If you see people approach, and there is nowhere to go, then give your dog a job by scattering treats on the floor near you to find. Don't let strangers approach your dog and pet them, as the attention can be too stimulating for your dog and they cannot make good choices when highly aroused.

Remember

Keep calm; your dog will take their cue from your emotions. Make sure everyone who comes into contact with your dog is following instructions. It only takes one person to disregard the new rules to undo all your hard work and training. Manage the situation, and be consistent. Your dog may not be perfect on every occasion, but the jumping up will be barely there most of the time.

Hopefully, there are some techniques and games here to encourage your dog to do anything other than jump up.

7

SEXUAL MATURITY, NEUTERING AND HUMPING

Have you ever wondered when your puppy technically became an adolescent?

One main school of thought is when their adult teeth come through and they no longer have needles in their mouth. Adolescence doesn't start the day after their final tooth arrives, but can be at any time from then.

As we found out in Chapter 1, their hormones start to change, and the brain initiates a whole host of tweaks and improvements within their bodies, not stopping when their legs stop growing but for some months afterwards depending on the breed and size of the dog.

And we also revealed that they are sexually mature a long time before they are emotionally and socially mature.

Despite them still being very puppyish in their approach to life, they can be a parent. Scary. Even though they are not mentally or physically in the best position to raise a family.

This time of their lives raises many questions, and no one answer fits all dogs. As with everything, you can look at this subject from a medical point of view, or a behavioural point of view, and you still won't have the perfect answer. However, vets (medical viewpoint), behaviourists (behaviour viewpoint), and vet behaviourists (can see both viewpoints) do have the scientific knowledge to help you make more informed decisions than those based on anecdotal chat on social media. Be careful where you get your advice from, as when it comes to neutering, spaying or having entire dogs, everyone has an opinion. In this chapter, I am not in a position to give you definitive advice on your exact situation, but to highlight some aspects so that you can ask relevant questions to the right qualified professionals to make a more informed decision.

Spaying and Neutering

This can be a very personal decision and is irreversible. There may be instances when this is necessary, but maybe you want to breed from them or show them on the pedigree circuit and they need to be entire.

Sexual Maturity, Neutering And Humping

Not every female dog needs to have a litter of puppies. Pregnancy and birth can be traumatic for them, and raising a dozen pee/poo machines is harder than you think. You may have to bottle-feed them every few hours, for a month or more. To help them become wonderful pets, you need to do more than just leave it to mum. Enrichment, exposure, and development are vital long before they get sent to a new home. From the moment of conception, any stress on the mum can hugely impact the puppies and their temperaments. If you plan to go down this route, do your research. Even the matching process needs careful planning as you need to not only consider the health of each parent but temperament too.

If you don't fancy breeding from your dog, then you may consider spaying (for females) or neutering (for males). Living a life of raging hormones and frustration can be challenging for them, and some dogs may need to be neutered for medical reasons. Some may need to be left as they are (called intact or entire) for medical reasons too.

It doesn't magically change their behaviour and is not a replacement for training. It can however help your dog focus better on you and not be constantly scanning for a mate.

As we saw in Chapter 1, many of the development hormones are switched on by the sexual hormones. Testosterone in both males and females is considered the main confidence hormone. Stopping this supply if your dog has anxieties will not help them much.

If you plan to neuter, consider the timing carefully. Many vets will give a blanket age they will operate on based on the size of the dog, and often once their legs have stopped growing. But a teenage dog's bones are still forming, and their brain has only just started to develop. Cancelling the hormones too early can affect their behaviour. Just as it will affect their medical health.

There is no perfect time, and there are varying impacts based on medical or behavioural viewpoints. Breeds, size of the dog, general health and much more will make this a very grey area regarding when to neuter. There are pros and cons to health and behaviour whether you go ahead when they are young or wait until they are older. The only thing I can say is to do plenty of research, look for second opinions (not from keyboard trolls on social media), and go with your gut. Don't be forced into anything unless it is a medical emergency.

Even how they are neutered can vary from one vet practice to another, as it could be a full incision surgery or keyhole. Your dog, recovery time, and affordability all come into consideration.

Don't be pressurised. This can be hard to apply, as many group dog day-care centres or boarders will not take entire males after age 1. Many dogs are still puppies and not even close to being adults, and you are being asked to switch off their development hormones. It may be harder work for you in the long run as they are immature for longer (who can say if they can be 100% mature?) but you need to balance your needs and that of your dog.

Seasons in Females

Females generally come into season twice a year, and seasons start from age 6 months or even as late as 30 months – each dog is different. Some dogs are badly affected by their seasons and need medical help. Keep in touch with your vet.

Seasons are generally 2-4 weeks long. The first week is your dog's body preparing itself, they will bleed at this stage and they are at their most fertile. She may be feeling under the weather, less tolerant of dogs and then very interested in them, have a swollen vulva, weeing more than normal and can be anxious and nesting. They can be sensitive to your touch or grumpy with you.

Even though the bleeding may stop, your girl is still very fertile, and care must be taken for the full duration of the season. Don't leave them unattended even in the garden, keep them on lead and if you do have to take them out, avoid busy dog parks. Every male will be noticing her from a huge distance, and even neutered males can do the deed – they just fire blanks and can't get her pregnant, unlike entire males. Other females may react differently to your dog at this time so it is better to not take your dog out at all. Instead, give them lots of puzzle toys, find-it and brain games, skills training, and teach them new tricks if they are willing – anything to enrich them instead of upsetting every other dog and owner in the vicinity.

Whether your girl gets pregnant or not, they then still go through the full hormone cycle as if they were, which is why vets will not spay them for 3 months since the last season. The prolactin hormone is present for this time after the season, and if spayed during this time then even medical intervention will struggle to stop the state of persistent phantom pregnancy.

In some dogs, the season is not always obvious, so if you think it may be that time of year, take precautions so that you avoid any unwanted pregnancies.

Keep your female dog away from resident male dogs, and avoid group training classes for these weeks.

False or Phantom Pregnancy

A phantom pregnancy may occur regardless of whether she was mated during her season. You would likely spot the first signs a few weeks after her season when your bitch may display nesting behaviour and will often carry toys or random items around as if they were her puppies.

This can be a stressful time as often females will produce milk as though feeding puppies. Phantom pregnancies will generally resolve on their own after two to three weeks. However, when a female has suffered from this condition once it is likely it will happen again. Neutering is the recommended course of action but speak to your vet first.

Chemical Castration

For male dogs, rather than undergoing full surgery, there is an implant that switches off the sex hormones for a set period. Once the implant stops releasing the chemical then your dog is intact and can get a dog pregnant. In adolescent dogs, this may sound like a good option but be aware that you are still stopping the key hormones during development. You cannot pause the brain like pausing live TV, and then thinking you can just run the programme later and all will be fine and restart once the implant stops. It still interferes with hormone levels.

This could be a good option for older teenage dogs or adult males if you are uncertain about the full neuter surgery, and want to see the impact on them both physically and mentally first. Again, do your research and speak to your vet.

Humping

Dogs will hump other dogs, humans, other animals, objects, pillows – in fact, anything. It may be just a few seconds or longer, and it can be embarrassing watching this happen.

Humping is normal behaviour. Both males and females mount and can start from puppy age, particularly during play. Your dog is not abnormal.

As well as reproduction, it occurs in many other contexts and emotional states. Dogs mount when they are excited and aroused, stressed and anxious. It can also be a displacement behaviour – something that occurs to take the pressure off or to show conflicted emotions. An example would be visitors to the home causing excitement and stress together, or if they are bored. During play, it can be attention-seeking behaviour or if they are overexcited. It can release a build-up of hormones, just as a cup of tea or biting our nails help us and our arousal levels. Dogs may hump due to a urinary tract infection so get a vet check if this is a concern.

It's common to hear owners refer to mounting as dominance, but in reality, studies have shown that this is not the case; it doesn't have much meaning at all other than it feels good to them. There is not enough research to find out if it happens more when other dogs are around, so it is more a show of posturing than any other meaning, but this is commonly speculated.

Mounting is normal and we should let dogs be dogs, we really should only be concerned if it is becoming a compulsive habit, an addiction.

If the humping is frequent and becoming a problem, make a note of when your dog starts. Is there any pattern that you can see? Maybe after a game of chase with a friend, or a strange dog barks loudly at them. Both these scenarios raise their arousal levels, and hormone levels. Dogs have a few tactics to make themselves feel better. Some do a full body shake, and some hump. Keep a diary and make notes of what happened before so you can be prepared.

If your dog is prone to spinal issues such as IVDD in Dachshunds, then do break their habit as soon as you can.

Interrupt your dog before they try humping, and distract them with a treat, a game of tug or retrieve, or a trick they know. You are aiming to reduce their stress level and teach an alternative behaviour. If there is an environmental trigger, move away and create a safe distance for your dog. Distracting them before will break the cycle better, and depending on what caused the humping, see if you can stop the play earlier, or work on their confidence around other dogs. Do get an accredited trainer to help you with games and tactics if their humping is bad.

Just to clarify

Spaying and neutering is a personal decision, and one where you need to get good advice from your vet, and accredited behaviourists as the impact on both their long-term health and behaviour can be long-lasting. Each dog is an individual. What works for one dog may not be appropriate for another. I have written a brief outline of what to expect but do your own research before you make your final decision. Neutering is not a solution to change their behaviour, but it may help their focus for you to address the running off, increased aggression, or whatever it is you are hoping to change. It's not my place to tell you what to do here, however, I hope that it raises some questions for you to ask the medical professionals.

8

OBJECT GUARDING

Sometimes your dog doesn't want to give up what they have. They perceive it as high value and don't want you to steal it from them.

But it can be an object they are not allowed, or not safe to have, or a space or person they are inclined to guard.

Has your dog created a game to get your attention by grabbing your things and you chase them, or have they learnt that you often steal or snatch items away from them, making them feel that your hands near them are threatening – their viewpoint, not your intention?

Guarding can become a real problem; at its worst, dogs can bite to protect their possessions. Prevention is better than cure, however, if your dog is showing early signs of guarding, then there are exercises you can do to help everyone in the family.

If your dog is extreme in guarding or has bitten, get advice first from a clinical behaviourist before trying these exercises, as sometimes there is a deeper emotional reason that needs unpicking before you start training.

As with any dog behaviour, if this is a sudden recent change in them, it could be related to pain or discomfort and a full vet check is recommended to rule out medical reasons for guarding.

Look at everything (or everyone) your dog guards. Is it just some specific items, or lots of things? Can you see if their reaction varies depending on the item? If more than one, then work on the least worse reaction first. Build up to the most challenging possession. I will discuss food and toy guarding in this chapter, but if they guard people, then go to an accredited clinical behaviourist for further advice and support.

Management

Safety is paramount, and firstly you need to make sure your family are up to date on spotting anxiety and stress body language (See Chapter 3 for more on this). Can you ensure that offending items are out of your dog's reach? If they cannot reach or see the item, they are less inclined to guard it.

Use an exercise pen opened up to separate your dog from the children's toys – you can all be in one room but you and your children will be safer.

Despite any frustration or annoyance you feel, you need to abstain from grabbing your dog, manhandling them, snatching an object, scolding or shouting at them. This can be our automatic reaction but your dog is only learning that if you come close, put your hands near their mouth, or become loud and scary, they will guard it, even more, to keep you away. And this can result in growling, snapping and biting.

I normally recommend to my clients that unless their dog has something that can kill it (such as a knife), then everything else that can be replaced is collateral damage. Put it down to learning and do your best to keep the offending objects out of reach. Use stairgates to limit access to bedrooms if your dog tends to steal toys or clothes from there.

If they cannot practice the behaviour, then you can work on changing their habits and emotions to more appropriate things to focus on.

Food bowls

Make sure your dog can eat in peace away from people and other resident pets. This could be for their dinner or any tasty chews given to them. Food is highly prized, and they only have access to this when we choose to feed them, making it even more special.

I have been asked to 'teach a dog to get used to someone taking their dinner away before they have finished'. My response is to think about what you are asking them. I will get very annoyed (probably beyond annoyed) if it's my favourite dinner and your dog should not have to go through this frustration either. If you are concerned about children, then ensure that the dog is not disturbed when they are eating. Keep your children away.

There is no need to have your hands in their dinner. Watch their body language if you move around the room when they are eating. Do you see them freeze, or gulp their food faster? Often you see them stop but they watch with a sideways glance and show the whites of their eyes.

You can teach them that you are not a threat to their meal, by ensuring you are at a distance that is not disturbing them or stopping them and throwing tasty treats at the bowl. Boiled chicken is a firm favourite for most dogs. Keep your distance, to begin with, and over time, build up to stepping slightly closer. They learn to associate your hands with bonus food and will tolerate you moving around the room better. Do not go so far as to touch or move their bowl, this stage is unnecessary as you do need to let them eat in peace. They should be eating at their normal pace so if they stop or go faster, then you are too close, go back a stage and build up slowly.

Special spots on the sofa

Dogs love the comfort of the sofa and the heat from where you have been sitting. If they get upset about being asked to move, first check if you are being consistent about whether they are allowed on it. Dogs prefer clear boundaries, so decide if they are on the sofa at any time, or not at all. Making up personal rules about timings means nothing to a dog who cannot tell the time. If someone allows them up, and another household member doesn't, this confuses your dog. Have one rule of yes or no, and stick to it for everyone.

It may be tempting to grab, manhandle or shove your dog off the cushion. This can make them wary of you approaching them. Rather than punish your dog, teach them an alternative that they can do. The Magic Mat game in Chapter 4 encourages your dog to love the mat and makes lying on that spot more worthwhile as you will be actively rewarding them for staying there and settling down to relax.

Sometimes they may not move onto the mat (you need to top up the magic by practising more), and so the Nose Touch game moves your dog around without needing to lift or shove them.

Nose Touch

You will need treats, and a clicker (or use your marker word).

1) Make the palm of your hand smell of the treat by holding it for a minute.

2) Have your dog sit close to you.

3) Present your flat hand to your dog. Hold it about 2 inches from their face to the side of their mouth. Avoid having your hand directly in front of their nose and don't shove your hand onto their noses – no tapping them.

4) They should turn their head to smell the palm of your hand. The instant you feel their nose touch you, click (or mark) and follow this up with a treat.

5) Present your hand another 5 times so they get used to bopping their nose on your hand.

6) Now present your hand another inch away, so they need to stretch their heads a bit further.

7) Introduce your cue – I use 'touch'. Now present your hand again. Remember to mark and treat each time they touch you.

8) Increase the distance gradually so they have to move further each time.

9) If they get stuck and do nothing, either stop because they are getting bored, or reduce the distance to get to your hand.

Using the Nose Touch game to get Reba off the sofa – action shot!

Keep the training sessions short. In no time at all, you will be able to get your dog racing across the room, or in from the garden for a Touch cue.

What to do if they have taken something

How to deal with this all depends on the context, and what your dog has learnt. Our first natural reaction is to stop what we were doing and move to the dog. They start to run away and before you realise what is happening, your dog is having a great game of chase as you fly around the room after them. They can even learn which items instigate the game – maybe a sock or the remote elicits more chasing than the newspaper.

Next time, do nothing. Ignore your dog. The caveat here is if they have a history of swallowing items, or it is unsafe, then of course you need to get into action. I'm giving the example of a safer stolen item. If you are no longer chasing them, they will quickly get bored and give up. Now is the cue to get up and present them with an appropriate toy or chew. Most dogs do this if they are bored so check if they need some brain games or a walk, or if they need to settle and sleep. Or cuddles and attention but without stealing the slippers first.

The other option if you need to get the item from them is to teach a strong exchange. You guide them to learn that giving up the first item equals receiving another valuable item that they are allowed. How you teach this can depend on whether your dog is more food or toy motivated.

Toy swap

Have two identical toys – tugs or soft frisbees work well. While hiding one behind your back, present the other to your dog. Keep hold of it and play with your dog and have some fun. Let go of the toy, and your dog will probably move away from you with it. Ignore them and immediately bring out the second toy and animate it close to you. Put all your attention on the second toy. Ideally, your dog will drop the first and come and play with the second toy. Play with them for a bit and you can slowly move closer to the first (dropped) toy. You can even throw the toy away from you and as they chase it, go and pick up the first toy. Repeat.

Your dog is learning that by giving up one toy, they instantly get another game with you with the second one. Having the toys the same means they are of equal value to your dog, one is no more important than the other.

If the objects are not the same your dog may not be so interested in the second object. In this instance immediately give back the original item (only if it is safe to do so) several times before ending with a big finish, and hide it away. We want to teach them that relinquishing the toy does not mean that they lose it straight away. If they have taken contraband then get them interested in a more appropriate toy, and remove/return a few times in quick succession before ending the game.

Your dog may become excited and fuelled by adrenaline so keep these sessions short.

Food swap

This works best for dogs that value food over toys. Make sure you offer a decent amount of food of good enough tastiness to make your dog want to swap. Practice with lower-value toys or items first in a training session. Play with the toy, and when your dog goes to hold it, or just after they grab it, present your hand flat with food in the palm close to their nose. As soon as they let go of the toy or item, drop the food and let them drop their heads to sniff and snaffle the treats.

Again, they are learning to give up one object for really tasty treats.

You can teach a Drop cue by saying this as soon as they spit out the toy, and just before you drop the treats. In time and with practice, you can ask for a Drop and they should spit out the item.

Better still, distract them before they get to put their mouth on the item and reward them by dropping the treats on the floor for them. They learn to not even bother grabbing the object in the first place.

All these exercises take practice and perseverance.

Object Guarding

Start with easy items and gradually build up to everything they perceive as valuable.

Watch their body language at all times.

Safety must come first.

If in any doubt, get professional advice.

9

BITING AND MOUTHING

Your puppy used its mouth to explore the world, to find out what was edible, what was safe, and what it needs to avoid.

They will always explore us, but their needle teeth are painful. How we reacted to this has a big impact on teenage dogs, and if they still bite and mouth us.

Dogs mouth each other during play, and also if their gums hurt (especially during that teething period). But now your dog has their full set of 42 nashers, and its jaws are stronger, why are they still nibbling us?

Frustration

When they can't get access to what they want, which can be needing us to retrieve a hidden toy or needing to go out to the toilet, the frustration can lead to biting.

Overtired Or Overexcited

Teenage dogs need a lot of undisturbed rest and sleep each day. If they are overtired, then they just can't concentrate on anything and can use their mouths out of frustration. Getting overexcited has a similar result, they just can't think straight with all those hormones surging from the fun.

Creating Distance

Quite often, we want to touch our dogs a lot more than they like being touched. Even if we have introduced the pairing of hands with nice things, they may want to tell us to leave them alone and create distance between you and them. If you have a small dog, then this also happens when you go to pick them up (dogs don't like flying) or hug them (they don't like restraint). Instead, listen to them and give them their space when they ask. Do two strokes on their body and see what they do—if they do nothing, look or lean away, then leave them alone until later. Need to move your dog? Instead of lifting them, teach them a nose touch to your hand to get them to come to you.

Pain

Pain can manifest in many behaviours including excessive biting, and if you notice an increase in biting or guarding towards you, then get a vet to check out for discomfort or pain.

Unethical Training Methods

If you have used more punishment/telling-off techniques, then this can make things worse. Firstly, all the attention you are giving as a response can be perceived as rewarding – they have you looking at and talking to them. So they will bite again to get another attention response from you. Dogs don't understand the concepts behind our language either. Secondly, these methods can cause fear and intimidation, so your dog may bite back to create space from you. Science has shown that even if you think this is working, behaviours are suppressed and often reappear in more dramatic ways.

What Can You Do?

If you have ruled out teething, tiredness and pain, then think about how you may be inadvertently rewarding your dog with attention. How do you react? High-pitched noises, flapping arms and running around are just making your dog more excited – you look like the most amazing toy!

Set your dog up for success by making sure you are not wearing flappy clothing, and have treats handy for you to reward all the times that they do not have their mouths on your skin or clothes.

Keep play sessions short to manage their arousal levels, and sprinkle treats on the floor so they have their noses, and attention, elsewhere.

If they do go to put their mouths on you, stop moving, look away, and remove yourself from them – this could be climbing over a stairgate so they can't get to you. When they have calmed down, you can reward this by whispering platitudes, and maybe some treats on the floor. Re-enter the room and repeat if needed. They are learning that if their teeth touch you, everything stops.

Have plenty of good chews for them. Chewing is a natural behaviour, so the more they can chew safely the better. My girl loves the elk and antler chews, and the West Paw Toppl filled with tasty food. Natural chews are great too, the ostrich twists are low-calorie, and she loves the beef ones as well. I avoid the pig products as they are higher in fat, and I struggle to give her things with hair, but I'm sure she would love them.

Some breeds (eg Labradors) are bred to carry things, and a way to help them is to have some squishy soft toys for them to keep in their mouths. They can't bite you if their face is full of a soft toy.

Other breeds, such as terriers, love to 'kill and dissect' so cheap toys for shaking and de-stuffing (supervised of course so they don't eat the innards) will help manage their desire to use their mouths.

Remember to keep calm, find out why your adolescent dog is still mouthing you and take steps to reduce their opportunity to do so. Keeping their arousal level down, and ensuring they have good quality rest will help you enormously.

10

INDOOR CHALLENGES

At home, you hope that your teenage dog will adjust into a calm adult dog who can relax when you need them to, but engage and play with you when you have the time and energy.

Sadly, dogs do not easily fit into our routines. This means they can be boisterous, attention seeking and needy at just the wrong moments. You are in a small, confined space with all your family and frustrations can grow quickly.

Sometimes your dog cannot go outside for many reasons – it could be cold, dark or stormy outside, or they are on restricted exercise post-injury.

In this chapter, I will address a couple of common problems and suggest some indoor entertainment games that you can use if you cannot get them outside for a walk.

Counter Surfing

Dogs are naturally born to be opportunist scavengers. Even if you have just fed them, the temptation to go and look for food is strong. It gets even stronger if they are bored or frustrated. And most dogs can reach your kitchen surfaces or dining table. I never fail to be surprised by just how high a small dog can jump if there is a prize to be won.

It only takes one win of some tasty food for your dog to keep trying. Similar to a slot machine, once you have a payout, you are inclined to keep playing as you assume you must win more money soon. You are hooked. Same for your dog. One stolen sandwich is enough for the addiction of trying to get more.

Your first line of defence is management. Never leave food out unattended, the temptation will be too great. Ensure that every crumb is cleared away, and any food is in secure tubs or behind a cupboard door. For dining tables, you may need to make sure the chairs are always tucked under or even propped forward against the table so that your dog cannot climb on them to reach the table.

Indoor Challenges

If you are going to be cooking and prepping food, then have your dog on a long line held by another family member so they cannot reach you by the cooker. Or have a stairgate blocking access to the kitchen. In larger open-plan rooms, use an exercise pen to divide the room up into two – and your dog will be on the side away from the kitchen counters.

Next, and just as important, is to teach your dog what you want them to do instead, or where they should be. Just shouting at them doesn't work, nor does grabbing their collar and dragging them away.

The most successful game to play is the Magic Mat which was described in Chapter 4. Have the mat close enough, to begin with so you can easily throw treats onto it whenever your dog touches it. Don't prep food, make it easy for them by just standing by the counter where you would normally cook. Practice little and often. Slow down the rate of throwing treats so your dog learns to settle, and you can encourage them to stay on it longer by then giving them a chew.

You can gradually place the mat further away from the countertops, to a safe area that will enable you to carry pans of hot water around without tripping on the mat or the dog.

Add a cue of 'settle' once they are on the mat, and just before you throw the first treats. You don't need to keep saying it but your dog will build the association of the word meaning they need to lie on the mat.

Build the challenge by starting to prep food in front of them when they are on the mat.

The only way to be successful is to be patient and practice a lot. Do this each time you make a coffee, in between meals, and be prepared for some mistakes, to begin with when you do get food out. If this happens, encourage them back to the mat, reward them lots for going there, and try again.

Indoor Games

Staying indoors does not have to mean doing nothing with your dog. Even more so if you are unable to take them out due to females being in season, post-surgery restrictions, anxiety or bad weather.

Using your brain takes up a higher calorie consumption than physical exercise and the same is true for your dogs. A large chunk of your dog's brain is set aside for scent detection and therefore search games are wonderful to keep them entertained, and make them tired. Sighthounds see the world first, but all other dogs rely on smell as their main sense, but all dogs love to search. Utilise this wonderful gift they have and they will be very satisfied indeed.

With all these games, supervise your dog. Some may want to shred any cardboard but if they are inclined to eat the items, then remove the object as soon as they have found the treat. Have a party when they have found it, and sprinkle more treats on the floor a short distance away so you can go and get the objects without any fuss or guarding problems.

Game 1

Use treats, or split their dinner into a couple of small bowls and hide them around the house and garden. Ask your dog to 'find it' and off they go!

Game 2

Put a row of boxes and bags in a line, and add a treat to one of them, making it easy to access. Stand with your dog at one end and get them to find it. Watch them check out all the items to find the food. You can repeat this and place the food in a different box or bag each time. There may be residual food smell in the first object which will get their interest, so you can place the treat in the same box but swap it around with another to change its location in the line.

Game 3

Sprinkle treats or their dinner biscuits on a towel, and roll the towel up into a sausage shape. Your dog needs to work out how to unroll the towel to get the food.

Game 4

Have a shallow box and fill with toilet roll tubes standing on their end. Sprinkle treats or dinner biscuits over the box and let your dog work out how to remove the loo rolls to get to the food.

Game 5

Can you teach your dog to sit in a box? Teaching them new tricks can be great fun, really bonding for both of you and who doesn't love to show off a new skill? Use food by their nose and move your hand to encourage them into the position. Mark/click the moment they are close, or there, and give the treat. You may need to take it slow and reward stages of getting to the end goal, it just depends on your dog.

Game 6

This is great for building their confidence. Collect up a selection of boxes, and have some sideways, on top of each other, upside down – just a random pile. Scatter food over, in and on the boxes and let your dog explore. You can also use plastic boxes or other items without sharp edges, whatever is safe for your dog to explore or stick their heads in.

Indoor Challenges

This is in the garden – but can be played indoors too

If you don't want your dog to search for food, hide their favourite toys instead.

The only limit is your imagination, but do make sure that it is safe for your particular dog.

11

COPING OUTSIDE

Your angelic adolescent can become a devil dog outside, which can be embarrassing for you, or you may even resent taking them out for walks. Being outside can be very distracting for your teenage dog. They are getting a big influx of hormone changes, and these make your dog more confident to explore the world further away from you. They struggle to multi-task – if they are sniffing and looking elsewhere, they are unlikely to hear you calling them.

Often you may resent taking them out, so they get fewer walks and become even more frustrated. When outside, unexpected things will happen. In the heat of the moment is not a time to train your dog. Interrupt your dog, move away and when it is less stressful for you both, find a more suitable environment and teach your dog the behaviours you want from them going forward. If their reaction is mild then all you may need to do is to give them time to process and work it out for themselves.

This chapter will cover just some of the challenges you may face, but my main message to you is to go back to your basic training for lead walking and recall and manage your expectations during this difficult phase they are going through.

Socialisation

When your dog was a puppy, they had an initial fear period from 8-12 weeks old as they became more mobile away from their mum. It's an inbuilt safety mechanism to make sure they can learn what is good and what can be dangerous. We are also told that in the first few weeks you have your puppy, you need to expose them to everything around them. They are learning all the time and we want them to cope with life.

It can be a mistake to think of it as a numbers game. You may have been told to get your dog meeting one hundred dogs by the age of 16 weeks (or any kind of statistics like that). This could mean one hundred scary encounters that only teach your dog to be anxious.

Socialisation is giving your puppy exposure to a range of people, dogs, objects, surfaces, smells, environments and noises. It's allowing your dog the space and time to work out for themselves what these new things are. It builds resilience if they can investigate in their own time rather than us forcing them forward as we know what everything is. Having just one or two great people and dog encounters is more beneficial than lots of scary ones. This is where learning dog body language is really important, as we detailed in Chapter 3.

Your job of socialisation does not stop there.

Adolescent dogs go through more fear periods as they mature. Rather than one block of time, it is mostly like waves that come and go, but each dog can be different. It runs from about 6 months to 16 months approximately, and their ability to cope with stresses will vary over this time. What looked fine and safe yesterday could be the biggest monster tomorrow. They see things differently from when they were a puppy.

To help them, acknowledge this as part of their teenage phase and let them work through this in their own time. Stop and watch them as they investigate, or give them time to slowly creep towards the object as they build their confidence. They may get more fearful of new people and dogs.

You can help them by sometimes placing a novel item on your floor, such as a bag that wouldn't normally be there. Or (safe) objects from the shed. Gentle words of encouragement can go a long way, but don't force your dog closer than they are comfortable with. Maybe try some dress up with big hats, floaty scarves or bright colours.

If you have taken on a teenage dog that did not get appropriate socialisation as a puppy, then your dog may be less sure about new and novel things. It may take them longer to recover from the feelings of seeing something new but if it is all a positive experience, they will become bolder and feel safe. Gradual exposure, repetitions, rewards and noting their body language will help both of you and they will learn to cope much better in different environments in the future.

Choose who they can go and meet, rather than strangers approaching them uninvited, and be a bit more selective about which dogs get close to you too. Be their guardian and be guided by your dog.

Confidence In New Environments

Being outside can be disconcerting for some dogs, and more so if your adolescent is having a fear period. With the breeze comes all the smells, on the ground is a trace odour of everything and everyone that has gone past, and the noises around them can be deafening. Some dogs love a new adventure and end up being over-excited with all the stimulation. This can make them hard to handle or respond to you. Or they can be hesitant, nervous and overwhelmed.

Whichever is your dog, there are some games you can do that promote confidence in exploring where they are.

Let them sniff

Dogs view the world through their noses, and letting them sniff allows them to catch up on all the latest news and videos. Think of it as them scrolling through their social media. Sniffing has many benefits including making them happy as lots of good hormones such as endorphins and oxytocin are released.

Use a longer lead as dogs that have more room to sniff by being on a long line of 3m or more, or off lead, sniff 300% more than a dog on a short lead. Sniffing has been shown to significantly lower their heart rate, and you may have seen your dog put their noses down after a scary or stressful encounter. This is them making themselves feel better. The more intense the sniffing, the slower the heart goes. You may have also seen them do a big body shake – this also lowers the heart rate to a more normal level.

There are times when a dog has to be close to you to be safe, but if you can, let them put their noses down and take their time. The walk with them is for their enrichment rather than you getting to Point A as quickly as possible.

Magic Trees

Take a liver paste or plain squeezy cheese out on a walk with you. Spread some of the paste on a tree at their nose height and make a deal about finding it. As your dog is licking away, move to the next tree, spread the paste and again celebrate both of you finding it. Repeat.

The aim is for you and your dog to bond over finding the paste on the magic trees. It helps them absorb the environment without focusing on what could be spooky, and even make your dog want to be close to you which only helps their recall.

Parkour

Use the environment to allow your dog to climb on, clamber under, or spin around objects and obstacles. This could be front paws on a tree stump, balancing on a log, or going around bollards in a weave pattern. Use anything you can find. It can be urban or rural spaces, just go wild with your imagination.

If your dog is unsure, give them time to investigate in their own time. You can even mark and reward for slowly raising a paw on the object, and again for shifting their weight further on, and finally for putting a second paw on. If your dog is more confident, then hold a treat by its nose and slowly move them forward so the paws go on the surface. Don't rush this, as your dog will need to coordinate their legs and find their balance.

Maybe you can get the back legs on as well. Dogs are less aware of where their hind paws go and any games involving placing them use a lot of brain power and puzzle-solving. You can even scatter twigs and branches, and sprinkle treats amongst them so they have to walk amongst obstacles. You can do this in your garden too with broom handles, poles, hula hoops and more. Just make sure nothing can flick up to hit your dog.

Coping Outside

Going Past Moving Triggers

Your dog is a natural hunter, and therefore moving things are more easily spotted than static beings. Cyclists, horses, joggers, cars, squirrels and anything that moves will catch their attention. But it is not very appropriate to go and chase them. And it could even be scaring them.

If they are showing deep fear or aggression, then you need to find a clinical behaviourist to help you, but there are some basic games to use to help your dog cope with the environment. The exercises here are at the easy level, for mild reactions, but it could still be a starting point for you while you wait for professional support. These may not stop chasing, as more advanced games could be needed to get your dog to focus on you and break the old habits, but doing something to keep them occupied is better than relying on them to make their own decisions when their arousal level could be sky high.

Catch the Treat

When the trigger comes into view, have your dog on a lead and throw a treat for them. Use a gentle underhand throw, keep it level to avoid the need for them to jump up, and aim for the nose. If they catch it, great. If they miss, they get to put their noses down to find it. Win-win. As soon as the trigger goes out of sight, stop the game.

I used this game to stop my girl from going up to horses. She was allowed to look at the horse going past (I made sure they would slow down for us), but she very quickly turned her attention back to me to throw the next treat. Now, whenever she sees a horse, she comes to me to play the game. I don't always throw treats but sometimes I will – the surprise and not knowing when we will play keeps her focus on me.

You can do this for cyclists, joggers or riders. Sometimes there is not enough time or space to stop and play this game, and then you just need to encourage your dog away and create space from the trigger. Do what you need to make your dog safe, and more interested in you.

Middle

This is where your dog 'parks' themselves between your legs, facing the same way as you, while something goes past. It can be their safe zone and tucks them away nicely if a cyclist passes by. They are close enough to feed which keeps them there longer.

With a treat in your hand, hold it by their nose and let them follow your hand as you guide them around your leg, behind you, and then forward through between your legs. As soon as their head pops out in front, with their tail end still behind you, mark and release the treat.

For some dogs, going under you (through your legs) can be a bit scary so reward them for getting that little bit closer each time. Let them build their confidence.

After a few goes with food in your hand, then pretend to hold a treat. Use your hand gesture in exactly the same way, mark when they are between your legs, and then get your treat out of your pocket to give to them.

Now, as they are getting good at going into position without a food lure, start giving your cue word (I say 'middle'), then do your hand gesture. You only need to say this once before you guide them with your hand. Remember to reward them in position.

She is not stressed here, but licking squeezy cheese off her nose!

As my dog Reba has a long tail, I use this so that cyclists cannot accidentally run it over as it won't be sticking out on the path in their way if she was facing me.

Look At That

Dogs can be upset by things moving past them, and the way to make them feel better is to change how they feel. Changing emotions is hard work, and if your dog is having a really bad reaction to various bikes, horses, cyclists, people or more, then professional help is the way to go. For general reactions, or to try first, use this exercise.

The key is to be far enough away for your dog to listen to you. If they are barking and lunging, then you are too close. Step back and create more space. Read their body language and look for when they are less tense.

Part 1 is to reward for looking at the trigger. Every time they set eyes on it, mark and treat. The clicker works well for this exercise as it is quick to use. You may be clicking in very quick succession as your dog keeps looking at the trigger. Remember the treat each time too. You can also drop the treat so your dog has to avert their eyes to find the food. If they are not eating, then they are getting too anxious and you need more space.

Part 2 is to reward them for looking, then looking away. Let them look and wait for 3 seconds. If they continue to stare at the trigger, you are not ready for Part 2. However, if within that 3 seconds they move their gaze away – possibly at you as they think you have forgotten to mark them, then click the instant they stop looking at the trigger. So now you let them look, they look away and then they get rewarded.

At first, you reward them for looking and the trigger now means something tasty is given to them. Then you reward them for looking and looking away. In future, the trigger is less scary and they could start to move to you instead as the trigger means treats – or a game.

Part 1- reward for looking...Part 2 – reward for looking, and then away from the trigger

Slowly decrease the distance to the trigger. It will take time and this will depend on your dog, how bad they feel and what the trigger is. Get friends to help out so you can guide them to go into view, then out of view. Once the trigger has gone past, stop the game. It only starts again when the trigger is back in view.

Meeting Other Dogs

We expect our dogs to be social butterflies, but this is just not the case for most dogs. As your adolescent dog grows, they will become more selective about who they want to say 'hello' to, and who is in their inner circle of fun and games.

It can become more common for your dog to not want to play or be jumped on by every other dog. Don't think your dog is broken. It is just part of growing up. Help your dog by teaching them polite greetings, and getting them out of there if they are not comfortable.

Knowing dog body language is important here, as well as some manners and etiquette. Do go back and look at Chapter 3 to refresh yourself on the signs. If you come across a dog on a lead, then you want to keep your pup away. Talk to them, keep their attention and walk on by. The other dog will be on a lead for a reason and less inclined to play. It could be that they prefer space from other dogs (dogs in yellow are a key indicator of this), maybe they are recovering from a vet treatment, or the owner just wants some quiet time to bond or train them.

Some dogs will be their best friends, so enjoy watching them play, chase, and have fun. It endears me to see two dogs that not only enjoy each other's company but listen and respect each other and bounce off each other's cues. Maybe one stops to have a breather, and the other one will follow. If one shakes, the other does as well. Then they may start the games all over again. Know when your dog is having fun, and when they have had enough.

Most dogs will prefer a polite greeting. This is where each dog will bend around to sniff the cheek or the bottom of the other. If one of the dogs shows any anxious signs or tucks its tails under, then separate the dogs and move on. Politeness is a 2 second sniff and move on. Teach your dog a 'let's go' cue so you can break up the interaction and your dog is willing to move away with you.

To teach the 'let's go' and call your dog to walk away in a different direction, first practice indoors where there are no distractions. If you plan to do this off-lead in the future, then you won't want to rely on food. With strange dogs close by, it may not be safe to put your hand with treats into their faces as you do not know how the other dog will react.

However, to get started you will use treats but build up to your dog responding to the verbal cue. With your dog in front of you and facing away, reach forward and hold a treat under its nose. Move your hand so that they turn towards you, and as they reach you, you also spin around so you both end up facing the opposite way to the start. As you are doing this, in a super happy voice, say 'let's go'. Once you have both turned and can walk a step or two in the other direction, give them lots of praise and some treats.

Practice this outside, and then with dogs in the distance. Say the 'let's go' cue, turn and walk the other way, and then reach for the treat and reward your dog. Finally, you can practice this when your dog has quickly sniffed the other dog as a polite greeting. As long as you make it worth your dog's while to come away from the other dog, then all is good. Maybe the reward will be to let them go back to the dog for play – with the owner's consent and if both dogs look happy to do so.

Be mindful if you are letting your dog greet another when both are on a lead. There is nothing worse than dogs being stuck together because of the leads getting tangled. When we pull the lead, we inadvertently lift the dog's chest and this can be misconstrued by the other dog as unfriendly. Puffing up the chest is a precursor to wanting to fight. If you need to pull your dog, try and keep your end of the lead lower so you don't lift your dog.

Travelling In Cars

Some dogs can be nervous in cars as they are not keen on motion. Or a vehicle can have very unhappy memories for them if they have had to endure a long journey. If your dog is hesitant to get into the car, then make it more fun by playing the Sticky Ham game. Avoiding the exhaust area, stick pieces of ham on your car at nose height. Let them search around (on a lead if it's not safe to have them roaming near a road) and eat the ham they find. Processed chicken sticks just as well. You can reduce the number of pieces on the car which will make it more of a fun search, and the sniffing can build confidence around the car as well as engage the brain in pleasurable things. Open up the doors and have some ham on the inside where the dog will be during journeys.

Once your dog is happier to get into the car, start by just closing the door, and then letting them out. Next get in the car with them, followed by starting the engine before switching it off quickly. Finally, you can move the car. It may be just a few feet there and back initially, but soon you can work up to longer journeys. Some dogs travel best in the boot, and some in the back seat. Some dogs prefer to look out of a window, while others don't. Try different setups and see what works for your dog.

If your dog barks at everyone outside of the car, see if you can screen off the nearest window – only if this does not impede your driving vision. Have a passenger reward your dog as soon as a person/car etc approaches. The Look At That game described earlier in this chapter is perfect here but you will need help as you concentrate on driving.

Driving with dogs in cars can be a hazard if they are not secured, or could be deemed as distracting you. Penalties can be your insurance invalidated, a £1,000 on-the-spot fine, or up to £5,000 and 9 points on your licence. So no dog on your lap – yes, I see this lots.

To secure your dog, the easiest way is to get a seat belt clip to their harness – never directly onto their collar – or use guards or crates that are secured into your car. You want your pet to survive any crashes so it is worth the investment. The best way is to get an official crash-tested crate fixed into the car.

Many dogs travel better with time and age, but if this is becoming a serious problem and they get very sick each time, consult your vet for advice.

Walking Nicely On A Lead

There could be a whole separate book on just this topic. My best advice to you is to go back to basics. Start with practising indoors where there are the least distractions, and mark/reward your dog for standing next to you. This can be with or without the lead on them. Remind them that the best place to be is next to your foot.

Progress to taking one step away. It can be in any direction and mark the moment they move towards you. Treat them and take one step again in a different direction. This gets your dog watching where your leg goes, and it pays to stick closer to it as they get their reward there. Now can you do two steps? You can mix and match, with one step in random directions, and then two steps forward. Mark and reward each time you stop to change direction.

Now build in distractions and practice in the garden. If you can only walk forwards, then do mark and treat after every few steps. You want to keep your dog motivated and interested, not knowing when the treat will arrive for them. Their patience is not good so don't leave it too long. Now select a quiet area away from your home. This can be up and down your road or a quiet field. Keep the sessions short each time, but several times a day if you can. Manage your expectations and take it slow. It's a tough skill for many dogs and can take a long time to master.

Not all dogs like walking in a straight line – the gundogs bred to search such as spaniels naturally go from side to side, so if you have a safe, wide area, then zig-zag walking is much more instinctual for them. Some dogs however were born to walk in a long straight line and they will be much happier to go along a track or pavement in one direction only.

Having a slack lead is the goal, and making sure your dog loves being by your side

Try and get the walking great without the need to hang on tight to the lead. The more anxious you are, the jumpier your dog will be on the other end of the lead. I only introduce my 'walk nicely' cue after my girl can do a few paces next to me and the lead is slack in my hand.

It may be tempting to use slip leads, or other training aids thinking these will work. Normally the dog will pull to try and get away from the choking or pain. The only thing that has been proven to work is training, patience and practice. We cannot remember how long it took us to learn to walk and for a sustained time, so consider your dog has to go through the learning curve too. Build up to distracting environments and try and enjoy your walks.

Recalling Your Dog To Come Back To You

Ah, the Holy Grail of an adolescent dog. As soon as they lose some of their dependence on you and notice the world around them, you are doomed. Well, not really but their original cue of shouting their name and 'come' could no longer work. If you have been overusing their names to mean everything, then they may not even respond to looking at you.

There are numerous ways to teach a recall and not all ways will suit all dogs. Saying the same thing over and over again will not suddenly change their response to you, so it is prudent to have more than one recall method in your toolbox.

Going off and exploring is very self-rewarding. They will forget you are there. To stop them from practising this habit of finding their own pleasure, you need to keep them on a long line while you go back to training.

You may want to use a new cue word. When my cue of 'come' failed to get my girl running back to me, I trained her to a whistling noise. But then I kept forgetting to take the whistle with me so I started again with a different word.

Teaching a new recall cue

With your dog already in front of you, say your new word and place their dinner down to eat. No need to ask for a sit or a wait, just give your new cue and feed them their tasty supper. Do this every mealtime. Your new word will soon mean that they get a bonus feast at your feet. After a week, now start saying your cue word when your dog is further away from you indoors. They will soon find you.

Now you can start practising in the garden but offer a handful of treats once they reach you. Use their ultimate favourite treats for recall, it is such an essential skill that it must be their best food reserved just for this. If you are expecting them to run away from a game or fun, and back to you, then what you offer needs to be more than one measly crunchy biscuit. Maybe your dog loves tug so you can use this as their reward instead.

Build up slowly in ever-increasing distracting environments. If in doubt, have your dog on a line. I never will trust my girl around livestock or picnics. Despite all my hard work, I know that she will never be 100% reliable – she is a thinking, sentient being. It is better to be safe in these situations. I use a 3-metre lead attached to her harness, so she still has space to sniff but it is short enough for me to hold and manage the other end, stopping her from getting into fields of animals.

I have several recall methods, and I apply different cues to different situations. 'Reba come' may work in general places, but if this fails, I have taught her an alternative to her name – 'ready' – to mean look at me, and then I say 'go, go, go, go' repeated in an increasing crescendo until she lands at my feet. And I pay her in a handful of food scattered at my toes as for her, this is a much better reward.

To teach her the 'ready' cue, I say it in an excited tone and feed her a treat. She is looking at me so I repeat. After a few goes, I wait until she looks away and say it again. Her head flips around to me. Now I have her attention. Try this with your dog. If their name has become white nagging noise then this will certainly get their heads turning.

The 'go go' part is a one-syllable word that I repeat for as long as it takes her to reach me. If I stop calling when she is only halfway to me, she gets distracted and veers off. To teach your dog, start with just them being a step away. Then two steps. As with all the training, teach them indoors where it is easy and slowly build up to being outdoors in the park.

Remember, keep your dog safe, and if you cannot trust them, there can be many enclosed fields you can hire by the hour where your dog can run around safely without escaping. You can also use these fields if your dog is not keen on strange dogs; it makes their walk stress free and enjoyable for them, and you.

You want to enjoy taking your dog out, so be bold, be proud, and be safe. Take the pressure off yourself and them by only walking occasionally rather than every day if it is overwhelming for both of you and use the time to play games or teach a new trick at home instead.

12

WHERE TO GET MORE HELP, AND USEFUL LINKS

When your dog's behaviour becomes too much for you, do reach out for professional advice and support. You are not expected to be an expert, but an accredited trainer is just that. They have the skills, knowledge and experience to help you, without judgement.

Recognise when it is frustrating, overwhelming or stressful for you or your dog and where you need additional support and guidance. It's not admitting defeat but being proactive to make your life, and that for your dog, so much better.

Keep doing the same reaction/words will not change your dog's response and a trainer can come and help you and your dog decipher what is going on, and give you tips and training to make everything better for you both.

If your dog has a sudden change of behaviour, then the first thing to do is to get a full check-up at the vet. Tell them what has happened so they can do a full pain/gut assessment. The majority of sudden changes to your dog stem from pain or discomfort and can be resolved by medical assistance.

However, if your dog has a clean bill of health, then getting in a trainer or behaviourist will help you.

How To Find A Good Trainer Or Behaviourist

The industry is unregulated, which makes finding a decent trainer who knows their stuff and who can assist you a minefield. I will briefly go through what to look out for.

Trainers

Trainers are the ones who help you change a dog's behaviour by linking cues and actions to make your dog do something. Basic obedience covers recall, walking nicely on a lead, leaving an object, or participating in activities such as agility, hoopers, scent training or gun dog exercises. After obedience, many trainers specialise in just a couple of other activities – they cannot be experts in everything, much like a surgeon or university lecturer.

When choosing a trainer to help you, not all use the same methods or have the same values. As mentioned in

Chapter 2, some use techniques that can hurt, scare or harm your dog. Some may use outdated references to 'alpha', 'leader', and 'dominance' and insist it was all your fault for letting your dog on your bed (completely untrue). If they use slip leads, choke chains, prong collars (which have spikes on the inside), electric collars or shout at your dog, walk away immediately. If it doesn't feel right, then it isn't. There is no 'quick fix' to change behaviour so anyone claiming this is most likely using aversive equipment.

And not all courses provide the same level of competence in the trainer's skills either. Some are about money rather than standards or watching a video without any practical assessment to ensure the trainer has understood or implemented the learning. Now, there are exceptions and some fantastic trainers that have experience only, but I prefer to recommend colleagues who are proud and unashamed to be regularly assessed and happy to support their experience with certification. You will be in totally safe hands if your trainer has been accredited by the ABTC (www.abtc.org.uk) as they have to go through yearly checks and continued learning to maintain their credentials.

Clinical Behaviourists

Clinical behaviourists are the elite in terms of having the knowledge and skill to understand the emotional aspects that may cause behaviours, and can help change your dog's view of the world. They will specialise in fear and aggression where the risks are high not only to the safety of humans but often to determine if the dog can stay with their owners. Although anyone can say they are a behaviourist, only *Clinical Animal Behaviourists (CAB)* can use this term if they are fully qualified and accredited, and will only use reward-based training to change your dog's emotions for the better and not use aversive methods that may at best do a temporary fix.

To find your clinical behaviourist, go to the APBC or ABTC websites

www.apbc.org.uk

www.abtc.org.uk – look for the CAB title next to their names.

If your dog has anxiety or stress around other dogs and people, then one-to-one coaching is better than a class environment. Once your dog can cope better, then carefully constructed classes can help – get advice from the CAB/trainer before you book anything.

Product Recommendations

Natural Chews

In Chapter 4, I talked about healthy, natural chews to aid calmness in your dog with the added benefit of these chews also doing a good job of cleaning their teeth in the process. I do have an affiliate link to Friends and Canines (https://friendsandcanines.co.uk/?ref=Pippin) Code is 'Pippin'. I get a small commission for sake of transparency. Reba loves the chews!

Feeder Toys

I prefer the West Paw Toppl, the opening at the top to allow access to the treats is wide and is therefore suitable for larger dogs and flat-faced breeds, or any dog that can get easily frustrated if they cannot reach the end of the feeder toy. An online search will give you suppliers for these amazing durable toys.

Dicky Bags

Fed up with filled poo bags in your pockets? I love the Dicky Bag. A neoprene holder with a scent disc that clips to your belt loop – or the lead. No smells, no mess and handy so you can then have your hands free for the rest of the walk until you get to a suitable bin. Go to their website www.dickybag.com and use code 'PIPPINS' for a little discount.

Dogs in Yellow

Sometimes your dog needs a bigger space around them, and not have others rush up to them (dogs and humans...). A good way to alert others is to have your dog in a yellow vest or other yellow items. There is a growing awareness of dogs in yellow – not fool proof but it may help you. Have a look at the website to buy a lead or vest in yellow, to show that your dog needs space. It doesn't mean your dog is aggressive, but maybe they are shy, or you want to have time to bond and train your dog without constant interruptions. www.bellascollars.co.uk is the website for My Anxious Dog.

There are many more products that I could recommend – more can be found on my website (www.pippinpetsdogtraining.co.uk) and you may even find some affiliate codes within my blogs. Go and have a read.

All links were correct at publication. If any links do not work for you, then do let me know at;

jo@pippinpetsdogtraining.co.uk

ABOUT THE AUTHOR

Jo Sellers is an Accredited Animal Training Instructor with the ABTC, Certified Separation Anxiety Pro Trainer, Scentwork UK and UK Sniffer Dogs instructor and member of the Pet Professional Guild.

Although always loving animals, her career started in Customer Service, Human Resources and Firefighting, before moving to become a full-time Dog Trainer.

Pippin Pets Dog Training was established in 2015 at the same time her dog Reba joined the family. This cheeky Cocker Spaniel/Bichon Frise crossbreed led her to specialise in Separation Anxiety after helping Reba overcome her fear of being home alone.

Helping dogs overcome Separation Anxiety is a key part of her business and online support can be one-to-one or in a group course. Reba suffered terribly so finding the most ethical, humane and effective method was key and Jo is proud to have helped many other dogs cope better when owners go out.

Launching the Dog Separation Anxiety Awareness Day (30th September) was a big step forward in highlighting this common phobia with the aim to reach even more dog owners, and offer information so more dogs can be helped when home alone.

From walking dogs to running training classes, she has observed and taught hundreds of dogs of all shapes, sizes and breeds. She particularly enjoys the puppies, adolescent dogs and scent detection classes as well as helping many online clients with skills training.

Jo regularly studies and learns from other amazing professionals to keep up to date and learn new skills and techniques to provide her clients with the best support and guidance.

Dogs are part of our families, and Jo is passionate about everyone loving their dog as much as she loves Reba.

Find Out More

If you would like to work with me or find out more about the ways I can help you, I would love to hear from you.

Visit www.pippinpetsdogtraining.co.uk

You can access my blog and podcast via the website too.

Email jo@pippinpetsdogtraining.co.uk

Bonus Videos

If you have enjoyed the exercises and would like to see the videos to explain some of these games, then scan the QR code below. This will take you to a webpage for you to enter your email address, and you will receive the link to the videos.

It will also add you to my mailing list for my newsletter, updates and more, however, you can unsubscribe at any time.

You can follow and connect with me socially on:

- facebook.com/pippinpets
- twitter.com/pippinpets
- instagram.com/pippinpets
- youtube.com/pippinpets

Printed in Great Britain
by Amazon